Let's Meet Famous Artists

By
Harriet Kinghorn, Jacqueline Badman,
& Lisa Lewis-Spicer

Cover Design by
Steve Volavka

Published by Instructional Fair • TS Denison
an imprint of

 **Children's Publishing**

Authors: Harriet Kinghorn, Jacqueline Badman, Lisa Lewis-Spicer
Cover Design: Steve Volavka
Inside Illustrations: Jennifer Ellis

 **Children's Publishing**

Published by Instructional Fair • TS Denison
An imprint of McGraw-Hill Children's Publishing
Copyright © 1991 McGraw-Hill Children's Publishing

Send all inquiries to:
McGraw-Hill Children's Publishing
3195 Wilson Drive NW
Grand Rapids, Michigan 49544

Let's Meet Famous Artists
ISBN: 0-513-02050-0

4 5 6 7 8 9 PHXBK 08 07 06 05 04 03

INTRODUCTION

There are many reasons for studying and creating art. Through study, we can learn about the important achievements and talents of famous artists and their work. We can try to understand what they hoped to communicate to our world. By doing art activities that are related to these artists, we practice the skills of observing, thinking, and creating. We can attempt to put ourselves into their minds, hearts, hands, and eyes. Once we do this, we inevitably learn more about ourselves — and that can prove invaluable.

In writing this book, it was our hope to bring the beauty and knowledge of artists and their art to you, the curious child or adult, the student, the teacher, and the parent. Use the following biographies, activities, evaluations, bibliography, glossary, and extended activities to enrich your understanding of artists and their art. Use this book also to enrich your artwork and yourself as an artist.

We believe it is important to encourage lifelong learning opportunities that promote organizational skills, which better enable us to communicate, make comparisons, and solve problems. These lifelong learning skills, in turn, bolster one's self-expression and one's self-esteem through creative thinking.

It is our hope then that this art activity book will afford you many hours of creative thinking and learning. But above all, we hope that the readings and activities in this book make you more aware and appreciative, not only of these featured artists, but of the special artists—creative children—who participate in these art experiences.

> Harriet Kinghorn
> Jacqueline Badman
> Lisa Lewis-Spicer

TABLE OF CONTENTS

TABLE OF CONTENTS

SUGGESTIONS FOR PARENTS AND TEACHERS

1. Read the included biography to obtain background information on the specific artist. (For school use, the biographies may be reproduced on both sides of a sheet of paper, or the two sheets can be stapled along with the corresponding activity sheet to make a booklet on each artist). You may wish to read other articles and books on this particular artist and you may wish to consult the bibliography for pertinent titles regarding the artist of your choosing.

2. After reading some background information on the specific artist, do the corresponding project suggested on the activity sheet. Although we have made a specific project that relates to each artist, you or a child may have a different project to create that correlates with the artist. If you should decide to create a project other than the one indicated on the enclosed activity sheet, the evaluation questions/statements will coincide nicely with it. Since a child has the choice of writing on four out of the six questions/statements, the child does not need to respond to one that doesn't relate to his/her projects. The child need only respond to questions/statements which pertain to his/her creative project.

3. When the child/children have responded to the questions and statements on the evaluation sheet, you may want to share and discuss those responses with each other. Appreciate the variety of responses you will hear.

4. Remember art has many purposes besides being beautiful. Art can be the result of a personal expression, an emotional release, and/or a learning experience.

BACKGROUND INFORMATION

ARTIST: _____ NAME: _____

ABOUT AN ARTIST

Find and read at least two sources about the artist that you are studying at this time. The sources might be an encyclopedia, book, filmstrip, newspaper, magazine, or another reference book.

Title of Media	Where it was obtained

OTHER INFORMATION DISCOVERED ABOUT THE ARTIST

_____

_____

_____

_____

_____

_____

_____

_____

_____

_____

_____

Use the back of this sheet if you need more space.

Alexander S. Calder
1898-1976

Alexander Calder was a famous American sculptor who is best known as the originator of the mobile, a structure usually hung from a ceiling, or sometimes free-standing, in which various components dangle from the center component of the mobile on "arms." If you have a baby brother or sister, they may have a mobile of brightly colored animals dancing above their crib.

Alexander Stirling Calder was born on July 22, 1898, in Lawnton, Pennsylvania. He was called Sandy by his friends who always remembered him as laughing, joking or giggling. Calder had a very happy childhood. His father and grandfather were sculptors and his mother was an accomplished painter. Despite his artistic background, Calder was not yet interested in art as a young boy, though he did enjoy making things and toying with gadgets. As a young boy he liked to collect scraps of all kinds, from broken pieces of glass and china to leftover pieces of wire and metal. Because he had such a large collection of "treasures," Calder's mother gave him a chest of drawers in which to house his collection. He loved to make new contraptions out of his scraps and his contraption-making fortunately continued in his adulthood. In his youth he was also interested in typical boyhood pursuits: he liked sports and enjoyed spending time with his friends and family.

After completing high school, Calder attended the Stevens Institute of Technology in Hoboken, New Jersey, and graduated in 1919 with a degree in mechanical engineering. He was employed in various engineering jobs before he began taking art lessons at the age of twenty four. Then, rather than taking engineering jobs, Calder began working as an artist, doing illustrations for the *National Police Gazette* for which he covered prize fights and the circus. This was very important in his career as this marked the beginning of his lifelong infatuation with the circus.

In 1926, Calder moved to Paris, a very important city renowned for attracting the modern art world. While Calder was there, he made friends with many famous artists though he distanced himself from the rest of the modern art world. Calder did not follow in other artists' footsteps: he was an innovator and worked to please himself. He made toy-like wire and wood sculptures which developed into a miniature circus collection. This circus collection is now at the Whitney Museum of American Art in New York City.

Through Calder's friendships with the Spanish Surrealist painter Joan Miró, and later with Dutch painter Piet Mondrian, Calder became aware of the current modern movement in painting. This influenced his work and his work became more abstract. Calder became interested in the three-dimensional aspects of art —height, depth, and width—and later, when he began creating his mobiles, he believed that space (or time) was an essential fourth dimension to the mobile's structure.

In 1931, Calder began making his motor driven sculptures. Calder's friend, a French painter, Marcel Duchamp, named the sculptures "mobiles" as their movements, whether from air currents or motors, gave the sculpture a continually changing composition. Another friend of Calder's, Jean Arp, a French painter, too, named Calder's sculpture that did not move "stabiles." A year later, in 1932, most of Calder's mobiles were driven by air currents.

At this time Calder was also interested in making jewelry. He made a wire necklace for his mother and he made his own gold wedding ring when he married Louisa C. James in 1931. He designed and made many pieces of mobile jewelry, from miniature mobile earrings to bracelets and necklaces that each had many separate mobile components dangling from them.

Calder and his wife traveled extensively and lived most of the time in Saché, France, where Calder had a home and studio. The couple also kept a home and studio in Roxbury, Connecticut. Calder had annual exhibitions of his work and he became more and more famous for his mobiles, which became larger later in his career. In 1955, Calder visited India where he was inspired to create eleven mobiles.

Before he died suddenly in New York City, on November 11, 1976, Calder was still designing mobiles and experimenting with free-form drawing and paintings. Calder's mobiles are the American sculpture most widely admired all over the world, and motion was the most important aspect in all of his work. But to Alexander Calder, it was most important that art embody happiness.

Name: _____

ALEXANDER CALDER

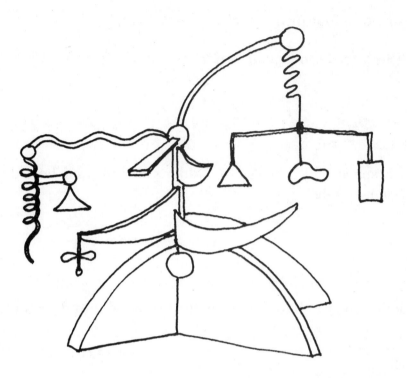

VOCABULARY: mobile, texture, space, three-dimensional, sculpture.

MATERIALS: craft wire, string, pipe cleaners, aluminum foil, markers, crayons, ribbon, paper plates, tagboard, and/or poster board, scissors, and any other suitable material.

ACTIVITY:

1. Study about some of the works of Alexander Calder.

2. Create a mobile from the available materials. You might cut shapes from paper plates or tagboard to make your mobile. You can color the shapes with markers or crayons or you might cover the shapes with foil to represent metal shapes. The foil can be colored with permanent markers, if you want.

3. Think about what parts you want long and what parts you want short. Think about how you are going to balance your mobile. Think about how the mobile will move when you hang it.

Evaluation   Name: _____

THINKING ABOUT CALDER AND ME

Respond to four or more of the following questions/statements:

1. Do you think that movement is part of Calder's art? Why?

2. How does space add interest to Calder's mobile and how does space add interest to your mobile?

3. Where will (did) you hang your mobile? Why will (did) you hang it there?

4. What is the name of your favorite Calder mobile? Why?

5. Write the name of one of Calder's mobiles. Then compare it to the one that you made.

6. Write one or more paragraphs about what you have learned about this artist and/or what you have learned through your own creative project relating to this artist. Write this information on the opposite side of this sheet, or on a separate sheet of paper.

Mary Cassatt
(kuh SAT)
1844-1926

Mary Cassatt was a highly accomplished and outstanding artist whose endearingly sensitive and subtle portraits of women and children crown the Impressionist art world. She is considered one of the leading members of the Impressionists, a group of painters working in the latter third of the 19th century whose paintings are characterized chiefly by short brush strokes of bright colors and experimentation with light and shadow which suggest—without fine details—the subject of the painting. Mary Cassatt is most famous for her intimate depictions of the tender and relaxed relationships between mothers and children. In Cassatt's paintings, often done either in oil or pastel, we see the figure of a mother quietly caring for her child.

Mary Cassatt was born in Allegheny City, Pennsylvania, on May 22, 1844. Her family was very wealthy. When she was seven years old, she moved with her family to Paris and they lived there for five years. While she was there, she became acquainted with the great art in the museums of Europe. When the Cassatts returned to the United States, to Philadelphia, Mary studied at Pennsylvania Academy of the Fine Arts. She found her studies there uninspiring, however, and she wanted to go to Europe, against the wishes of her family, to further her art studies.

When Mary was twenty two years old, she left for Europe and studied in France, Italy, Spain, and Belgium. She was especially influenced by the work of Correggio in Italy, Velasquez in Spain, and Rubens in Belgium, all very famous artists who were painting in the sixteenth and seventeenth centuries. Later in Mary's art career, she studied many Japanese prints and the Japanese art form greatly influenced her work in the 1890s.

Beginning in 1872, Mary began exhibiting her work in the Paris Salon. Edgar Degas, an Impressionist painter well-known for his graceful paintings of ballet dancers, very much admired Mary's work at the 1874 Salon and he invited Mary, who was now living in Paris, to show with the Impressionists. Mary officially joined the Impressionist group in 1879. The Impressionists were not very popular with the viewing public at the time because their painting style was so different from what the public was accustomed to. The public was unaccustomed to seeing so much vivid color.

Mary Cassatt formed a close relationship with Edgar Degas and both Degas and Edouard Manet were her mentors, wise and trusted advisors. Their technique and style greatly influenced and inspired Mary's own work. She was interested particularly in the effects of the light range of colors and the use of vigorous brushwork. Her own work, though, remains very original and outstanding both for its innovative technique and style, and she is considered one of the most consistently able American painters.

Mary concentrated on perfecting her vision of the human figure. She never painted a landscape and instead chose to paint the dignified working-class women who cared for their own children, rather than painting the upper-class women who hired nurses or nannies to care for theirs. Mary was interested in painting healthy and strong women, so her figures are of blunt-featured, sturdy women. Though children figure predominantly in her work, she had no children of her own. She often used her many nieces and nephews as models.

Because Mary was independently wealthy, she was able to pursue her career as an artist even though it was frowned upon as an occupation for women to pursue. She was, as well, an early feminist in thought and politics, and she championed the progress of women in the domestic world.

Mary's involvement with the Impressionists is very important because she introduced their paintings to the United States through her social contacts with rich, private art collectors. Mary also became a very well-respected art consultant. She would advise wealthy art collectors, like the Havemeyers, which paintings they should buy for their collections. Mary was instrumental in the formation of the Havemeyer collection, a famous collection of paintings.

Cassatt received France's Legion of Honor in 1904 in recognition of her dedication to her work. At that time, she was suffering from cataracts and losing her eyesight. Because of this, she abandoned her printmaking. She has left us a rich legacy, though, of approximately two hundred highly distinctive prints, perhaps her most original contribution to the art world. After 1914, now blind, she was no longer able to paint. She died at her beloved château near Paris on June 14, 1926.

Name: _____

MARY CASSATT

VOCABULARY: chalk pastel, technique, medium, manila or newsprint paper, delicate.

MATERIALS: colored chalk pastels, manila or newsprint paper (rough texture), cotton balls or cotton swabs, rolled tissue, finger tips.

ACTIVITY:

1. Study some of the works of Mary Cassatt.

2. Like Mary Cassatt, you will do a drawing with colored chalk pastels using a soft blending technique.

3. The subject of your drawing should be a person or persons expressing a positive emotion toward another person or animal.

4. You may want to show an adult expressing love to a child, a person being kind to an animal or an elderly person, or a young person sharing a pleasant visit with a friend.

5. Illustrate your subject using bright colors. Use cotton balls, cotton swabs, your fingertips, or some rolled tissue to blend the colors softly.

6. The roughness of the paper will hold the chalk nicely and allow you to blend the colors well. After blending, you can return to the drawing and add delicate details.

Evaluation   Name: _____

THINKING ABOUT MARY CASSATT AND ME

Respond to four or more of the following questions/statements:

1. Why do you think Mary Cassatt used chalk pastels when other artists at the time were using oil paints?

2. What medium do you like to use the most? Explain your answer.

3. Compare Mary Cassatt's medium and technique to Vincent van Gogh's.

4. Explain some of your feelings about your drawing.

5. Write a brief description about your drawing.

6. Write one or more paragraphs about what you have learned about this artist and/or what you have learned through your own creative project relating to this artist. Write this information on the opposite side of this sheet, or on a separate sheet of paper.

Paul Cézanne
(say ZAHN)
1839-1906

Paul Cézanne was the oldest, but one of the greatest, of the Post-Impressionist painters. While he associated with many of the Impressionist painters such as Monet, Renoir, Pissaro, and Degas, his vision and purpose in painting was quite different. Cézanne was a very intellectual painter, constantly searching for solutions to ideally represent his subjects. He was able to achieve great solidity and depth in his paintings and in his later landscape paintings, he was able to portray at the same time deep space and flat design. Cézanne always believed in the rightness of his art, even though throughout his artistic career he was constantly criticized.

Paul Cézanne was born to a very well-to-do family in Aix-en-Provence on January 19, 1839. His father, Louis-Auguste Cézanne, was a successful banker who wanted his son to follow in his footsteps. Cézanne's father was very domineering but he financially supported Cézanne throughout his career. Cézanne did enter law school at the University of Aix-en-Provence, but he had already determined for himself an artistic career. With encouragement and support from his mother, Ann-Elisabeth Honorine Auber, Cézanne's father finally allowed him to study painting in Paris.

Paul Cézanne arrived in Paris when he was twenty-two years old. He began his studies at the Atelier Suisse but became very depressed when he discovered he was not as technically skilled in drawing as the other students. He only stayed in Paris because his old school friend, Émile Zola, who eventually became a very famous writer, encouraged him. After five months, Cézanne returned to Aix to work in his father's bank for one year before returning again to Paris, determined to paint.

Cézanne was a very moody young man who did not make friends easily. He was very shy and sometimes rude; his behavior was very antisocial and because of this, he was very difficult to know. Cézanne eventually married Marie-Hortense Fiquet, the first woman with whom he had any relationship, but they frequently spent more time apart, than together.

In 1872, Marie-Hortense and Cézanne had a son they named Paul. Later in that same year, Cézanne and his new family moved to Pointoise in the valley of the Oise River. They were invited there by Camille Pissaro, a French Impressionist painter who had the patience and goodwill to teach Cézanne the techniques and theories of Impressionism. At Pointoise and the nearby town of Auvers,

Pissaro and Cézanne took their canvases all over the countryside and painted outdoors to fully capture the intense colors of nature and bright effects of sunlight. Cézanne used Impressionist techniques while emphasizing the form, solidity, and underlying structure in the objects he painted. Cézanne's use of geometric shapes laid the foundation for the later development of the art movement known as Cubism. He thought that everything in nature was modeled on three distinct geometric shapes – the sphere, the cone, and the cylinder – and he believed one learned to paint from studying those simple figures. Cézanne's work greatly influenced and inspired the Cubists Braque, Picasso, and Juan Gris in the early twentieth century.

Cézanne devoted himself to painting landscapes, still lifes, and portraits. He painted over two hundred still lifes, giving force and significance to simple everyday objects. He used very strong brushstrokes, simplified forms, and outlined with dark contours. The objects in his still lifes seem asymmetrical, or unbalanced, and this apparent lack of symmetry was always a deliberate and important component of Cézanne's work.

During the last six years of his life, Cézanne produced many masterpieces, including ten variations of one motif, a mountain called Mont Saint-Victoire. While the mountain in his Mont Saint-Victoire paintings is monumental and rigidly stable, the painting is alive with movement. Another motif, or theme, recurring in Cézanne's work included several versions of *The Card Players* and the *Bathers* series.

In 1895, Cézanne began to achieve fame and recognition for his work. While his work was admired for its important and novel contributions to the art world, much of the general public, and many art critics, believed Cézanne could not even draw.

On October 22, 1906, Cézanne, "the father of modern painting," died from diabetes complications prompted by a chill caught while working in the fields. A year after his death, an exhibit of fifty-six of his paintings was held at the Salon d'Automne in Paris where the collection won considerable acclaim.

Name: _____

PAUL CÉZANNE

VOCABULARY: depth, motif, symmetry, asymmetry, still life, recede.

MATERIALS: heavy paper or posterboard, tempera paint, or water color, or acrylic paint, brushes, pencil.

ACTIVITY:

1. Find and study photographs of Paul Cézanne's paintings.

2. Like Paul Cézanne, you'll paint an interesting still life painting.

3. You may choose to paint an arrangement of fruit or other objects.

4. When your subject matter is chosen, spend time arranging it. Look at the relationship between form, color, and positive and negative space. Are the objects right up front on the picture plane, or do they recede in space, creating depth?

5. Draw your picture first with pencil, then paint the still life. Sign your artist signature when you have finished with your project.

THINKING ABOUT PAUL CÉZANNE AND ME

Respond to four or more of the following questions/statements:

1. Describe the motif or motifs of your still life painting.

2. Explain why you chose your subject(s) for your still life.

3. Is the composition of your painting symmetrical or asymmetrical? Explain:

4. Why do you think such everyday objects like apples, tablecloths, and bowls became so important to Paul Cézanne?

5. If Paul Cézanne were alive today, do you think he would still be painting still lifes? Why or why not?

6. Write one or more paragraphs about what you have learned about this artist and/or what you have learned through your own creative project relating to this artist. Write this information on the opposite side of this sheet, or on a separate sheet of paper.

Marc Chagall
(shah GAHL)
1887-1985

Marc Chagall was a Russian-born artist who enjoyed reliving the memories of his childhood very much. He let his imagination shape and reshape his recollections of Russian folk tales and Jewish proverbs, of the countryside near his childhood home, and of his dear family and friends. Chagall included these fantastical images of reality, imagination, and dreams onto canvases splashed with bright and beautiful color.

Marc Chagall was born in the small Russian village of Vitebsk on July 7, 1887. He was the oldest son in a family of nine children born to Zahar and Feiga-ita Chagall. His father, Zahar, worked in a herring packing house, and his mother, Feiga-ita, sold herring, flour, sugar, and spices from a small shop in their home.

While at school in Vitebsk, Chagall studied the elements of drawing, and later painting, in the studio of a local artist. In 1907, when Chagall was twenty, he went to St. Petersburg (now Leningrad) to study with Léon Bakst, a brilliant stage designer. Then in 1910, Chagall went to Paris where he met many poets and painters later destined to become famous. With this creative and imaginative company surrounding him, Chagall was encouraged to paint the very poetic inner imaginings of his mind. Chagall said that it was the city of Paris itself that taught him more about life and art than any art academy or professor. To some viewers of his work, Chagall's paintings seemed irrational. Often Chagall included rooftop violinists (his favorite uncle was a violinist), upside-down and floating people, and animals with human features.

His painting entitled *The Birthday*, done in 1915, and now displayed in New York City's Museum of Modern Art, shows us Chagall floating into the home of Bella, his future bride. She looks as if she is about to float into the air, too, as she greets Chagall with a kiss and a bouquet of flowers for his birthday celebration. There is a cake and a slice of watermelon on the red table and outside the window we see a starry night and a quiet street.

The atmosphere of Chagall's paintings suggest the inner whimsical elements of a dream. Often times, the central figure of his paintings include a young handsome man looking very much like the painter himself.

In 1915, Chagall married Bella Rosenfeld, the daughter of a jeweler from Vitebsk, and her figure appears in many of Chagall's spirited paintings. After Bella's death in 1944, Chagall was unable to paint for many months. Bella's figure reappeared, however, in several Chagall paintings as a ghost-bride. Chagall married Vava Brodsky in 1952. Bella and Vava were the only people he painted portraits of after he left Russia in 1922.

In addition to his many paintings, Chagall produced many stage sets and costumes for plays for the Jewish writer Sholem Aleichem. He also did murals for the Kamerny Theatre in Moscow, and over a hundred etchings to illustrate Nikolay Gogal's book, *Dead Souls*, La Fontaine's *Fables*, and the Bible. The illustrations for these books launched Chagall on a long career as a printmaker.

During the 1920s and 1930s, Chagall's poetical painting became more popular. He traveled extensively throughout Europe but when World War I broke out, and as Hitler and the Nazis became more dangerous for all European Jews, Chagall took refuge, in 1941, with his family in the United States. He spent most of the next few years working in New York City, designing sets and costumes for the New York City's Ballet Theatre, and later for Igor Stravinsky's ballet, *Firebird*, and Maurice Ravel's ballet, *Daphnis and Chloe*, at the Paris Opera.

Chagall was also very fond of the circus and he paid homage to the circus through several of his paintings. Chagall believed that "...the circus is a magical show, like a world that comes into being and then is gone again." The magic in the circus is much like the magic in his paintings. In *The Large Circus* (1968) and in *The Grand Parade* (1979-80) – oil paintings which are both displayed in the Pierre Matisse Gallery in New York City – we see performers in the center stage of the circus arena, members of the audience, several musicians, including violinists, and large animals and floating people dominating the colorful canvas.

Chagall was a popular and leading innovator of the twentieth century school of Paris, and the huge flower bouquets, fiddlers on the roofs, floating lovers and angels, and animals with human-like characteristics dominate his rich, personal canvases. These dream-like and colorful images, reflecting themes from folklore, legend, and Chagall's own cherished memories, distinguish him as a master at conveying visual stories.

Activity Sheet   Name: _____

MARC CHAGALL

VOCABULARY: symbol, distort, hidden meaning, proverb.

MATERIALS: crayons, oil pastels, colored pencils, or colored markers, paper.

ACTIVITY:

1. Find and study some photographs of Marc Chagall's work.

2. Like Marc Chagall, you will create a brightly colored artwork. The subject might be a happy memory or a dream you have had.

3. Include symbols that mean something special to you. Include people and objects that are important to the memory or dream.

4. Try to draw it just as you remember it.

5. Feel free to distort something or someone if it helps support the meaning behind your artwork.

6. As always, sign your art with your special signature.

Evaluation   Name: _____

THINKING ABOUT MARC CHAGALL AND ME

Respond to four or more of the following questions/statements:

1. List the symbols you used in your drawing and define their hidden meaning (or what they mean to you in the drawing).

2. Why do you think artists use symbols in their work? Explain:

3. List the symbols Marc Chagall used and define their meaning.

4. Make up a symbol that defines who you are and put it in this spot.

5. Why do you think that distortion is sometimes used?

6. Write one or more paragraphs about what you have learned about this artist and/or what you have learned through your own creative project relating to this artist. Write this information on the opposite side of this sheet, or on a separate sheet of paper.

Edgar Degas
(duh GAH)
1834-1917

Edgar Degas is perhaps most famous for his graceful and soothing paintings depicting beautiful ballet dancers preparing to take class or performing on stage. Degas was a masterful portraitist and his many paintings and drawings (often done in his favorite medium – pastel), and bronzes, show us why he is the master of depicting the human figure in motion.

Edgar Degas was born in Paris, France, on July 19, 1834, to a wealthy aristocratic family. Degas' family had many banking and business connections both in the United States and Italy, and Degas seemed destined for the law, which he studied for a time. In 1855, however, he enrolled at the École des Beaux-Arts and began training in the tradition of Jean-Auguste-Dominique Ingres, a French Romantic painter whose masterful and powerful portraits unified the psychological depth and physical accuracy in his subjects. Degas learned much about portraiture through Ingres' influence, and it seemed as if Degas would become a painter of historical subjects in the grand French tradition of the time. But after much travel and studying in Florence, Assisi, Rome, and Naples, Degas slowly abandoned historical painting.

After 1861, he soon found his subject matter in the lively city of Paris, painting scenes from the world of entertainment. He was much inspired by the contemporary artists Gustave Courbet and Edouard Manet, and by the works of Japanese graphic artists. He was also interested in the camera and he became an amateur photographer. Often his work suggests a "candid" photograph, capturing the human subject unposed. Degas painted scenes from the Parisian dance halls, race courses, cafes, concerts, and theaters. He painted the participants and the spectators, figures engaged in their practiced movements, or figures engaged in solitary repose. Degas portrayed only people with whom he had emotional ties, particularly his family and friends, and through this, he developed a profound sense of human character. Degas enjoyed painting people involved with their work, whether he portrayed two women ironing in *Les Repasseuses* (1884-85), three ballet dancers in the process of adjusting their costumes in *Dancers Preparing for the Ballet* (1880), or a woman examining a hat in the *Millinery Shop* (1882). He was simply fascinated by people practicing their professions.

While Degas had abandoned his early pursuits of historical figure painting, he still put to use the technical skills and structural principles of the formal tradition. He was known as one of the most fastidious painters of his century and because of his high standards of quality he always tried to recover work with which he was unsatisfied. By the end of the 1870s, Degas became more interested in the possibilities of space between the figures he portrayed on canvas, giving more attention to the voids between the figures. After 1880, Degas began working on small bronze sculptures of dancers, bathing women, and horses. In these bronzes, as well as his paintings and drawings, Degas' mastery is at work, revealing to us the beauty of ordinary movements in human beings and horses. He was most interested in movement and the patterns that movement suggested against a background.

Degas' eyesight failed later in his life and he became almost completely blind. His drawing lines became less precise but his brilliant yet soft colors – produced by the use of pastel – became more intense. He died in Paris on September 27, 1917, full of self-doubt and a sense of failure about his work but leaving behind for us what was – and is – an invaluable collection of his art.

EDGAR DEGAS

VOCABULARY: sketch, gesture, figure, motion, accent.

MATERIALS: paper, colored chalks, pencil, colored pencils.

ACTIVITY:

1. Find and study some photographs of Edgar Degas' work.

2. Observe people in motion. Watch them dancing, jogging, building something, doing housework, and so forth.

3. Draw the figures in motion using a gestural sketch. Don't try to be too detailed. Suggest the human form in motion.

4. Once you have sketched in your figures, color them. Use the same gestural manner you used when drawing the figures.

5. Use color to accent the figures' motion.

6. The more of this type of drawing you do, the more you'll improve. Take your drawing supplies with you when you travel and do motion observing and sketching.

Name: _____

THINKING ABOUT EDGAR DEGAS AND ME

Respond to four or more of the following questions/statements:

1. Which do you prefer to do, a loose gestural sketch, or a detailed precise drawing? Explain:

2. Show your drawing to a friend, family member, or a teacher. See if their reaction to your drawing matches what you wanted the drawing to say or mean.

3. Do you think movement is exciting? Why or why not?

4. Describe a scene of movement you would like to observe.

5. If Degas were living at this time, what kind of artistic work do you think he would be doing today? Explain:

6. Write one or more paragraphs about what you have learned about this artist and/or what you have learned through your own creative project relating to this artist. Write this information on the opposite side of this sheet, or on a separate sheet of paper.

Albrecht Dürer
(DYUR uhr)
1471-1528

Albrecht Dürer was one of the greatest and most influential artists of his time. He regarded his profession as an artist very seriously and spent much time perfecting the painstaking detail in each of his drawings, water colors, oil paintings, woodcuts, and copper engravings. Dürer used his pictures to tell stories, and it was through his artistic and magical intensity of detail and precision that we know so much about the period in which he lived.

Albrecht Dürer was born in Nuremberg, Germany, on May 21, 1471. Dürer was one of eighteen children born to the goldsmith Albrecht Dürer the Elder, a very fine craftsman and scholar. Albrecht's father carefully trained him in the craft of making beautiful jewelry, but Albrecht decided at an early age to pursue a career as a painter, rather than a goldsmith. Albrecht's earliest known oil painting, completed in 1490, was a portrait of his father. This large portrait, showing his father as a strong yet gentle man, now hangs in the Uffizi Gallery in Florence, Italy. Albrecht's mother, Barbara Holper, was the daughter of a goldsmith. Albrecht's most expressive portrait drawing, now in a German museum, is of his mother.

When Albrecht was only thirteen years old, he drew a self-portrait in which his genius and skill for detail are already evident. He was the first artist to be fascinated with his own image and he produced many self-portraits throughout his career.

Albrecht's first works exhibit a tradition of art known as Late Gothic, a term which refers to the expressive style of painting and sculpture produced between the thirteenth and fifteenth centuries in Northern Europe. Late Gothic art is characterized by a tendency toward realism and interest in detail. After journeying to Italy to study, in 1494, Albrecht's work became greatly influenced by the growth of the Renaissance spirit. The Renaissance period overtook the Late Gothic in artistic style, becoming a time of great renewal in art, literature, and learning in Europe. The Renaissance period began in the fourteenth century and continued on to the seventeenth century. The word "renaissance" comes from the French word which means "rebirth." This period marked the transition from the medieval world to the modern world. Albrecht embraced the Renaissance spirit and can be said to have been a true Renaissance man. He was a great gentleman and scholar and confronted life to the fullest. His love for knowledge was as intense as his love for painting.

Albrecht married Agnes Frey, the daughter of a merchant, in May of 1494, and soon afterwards, made his first trip to Italy to study and paint. Many of the works by Italian artists influenced Albrecht's own work and he was much inspired by the work of the Florentine artist, Antonio Pollaiulo, and the Venetian artist, Giovanni Bellini. Albrecht's work adopted a more classical and humanistic approach, and he was quickly developing a reputation as a master of fine detail.

Albrecht made his second trip to Italy in 1505, and he remained there for two years, spending most of his time in Venice, which was a great center for the Italian Renaissance movement. Albrecht considered Italy his artistic and personal home and while there, produced many portraits, as well as a magnificent altarpiece for the funeral chapel of the Germans in the church of St. Bartholomew in Venice.

While Albrecht learned much about classical technique and style from the Italian masters, his graphics, in turn, greatly influenced the art of the Italian Renaissance. He was regarded as the greatest printmaker of his time and he had a wide influence on sixteenth century art through his woodcuts and copper engravings which surpassed standards of classical excellence.

Albrecht returned home to Nuremberg in 1507. In 1512, the emperor Maximilian I enlisted Albrecht to work for him. Albrecht worked mainly for the Emperor until 1519, producing drawings for his prayerbook, monumental woodcuts, and several portraits. By 1515, Albrecht had achieved an international reputation. He had traveled and studied throughout Europe, most notably in Italy, Germany, Switzerland, Belgium, and the Netherlands, where he maintained close relations with the Netherlands' leading painters.

After his final journey to the Netherlands with his wife, in 1520, Albrecht's health began to decline. He died in 1528, an artist aware of his intensely inspiring and influential genius.

Name: _____

ALBRECHT DÜRER

VOCABULARY: engraving, realism, texture, precise, intensely.

MATERIALS: photograph or picture of a real animal, paper, pencil, crayons.

ACTIVITY:

1. Study some of the works of Albrecht Dürer.

2. Observe a photograph or a picture of a real animal for at least three minutes.

3. Do a careful and realistic drawing. Study and draw as much detail as you can. (*Consider the texture, including fur, claws, musculature, and smoothness.*) Try to copy the texture of the animal.

4. Observe the color and the direction of the light on your drawing. Try to match the colors as you see them. Take your time with this project.

5. Be patient like Albrecht Dürer. Make your drawing an enjoyable project rather than a chore. Remember to sign your work in your own special way.

Evaluation   Name: _____

THINKING ABOUT ALBRECHT DÜRER AND ME

Respond to four or more of the following questions/statements:

1. What were you feeling when you were drawing so intensely?

2. Did you ever feel like quitting when the drawing got difficult? Explain:

3. Why do you think it is sometimes good to be attentive to details?

4. Tell in your own words why you think Albrecht Dürer worked so hard on including every detail in his artwork.

5. List some other people you know who do very detailed and precise work. Explain:

6. Write one or more paragraphs about what you have learned about this artist and/or what you have learned through your own creative project relating to this artist. Write this information on the opposite side of this sheet, or on a separate sheet of paper.

Edward Hicks
1780-1849

Edward Hicks was a nineteenth century Quaker minister and the artist of seventy known "Peaceable Kingdoms." The concept of a peaceable kingdom is based on an Old Testament prophecy. The prophecy says that in a peaceable kingdom, the lion will lie down with the lamb and a little child will lead all creatures. Hicks painted many versions of the Peaceable Kingdom and his 1824 *Peaceable Kingdom* is one of the most famous because the painting is so serene. Because he was a Quaker, Hicks believed in a gentle peaceful world where everyone could live in harmony.

In all of his paintings using the Peaceable Kingdom as his subject matter, Edward Hicks tells two stories. In one part of Hicks' Peaceable Kingdom paintings, he paints a Biblical story; in the other part of the same painting, he paints a historical story. And in all of Hicks' Peaceable Kingdom paintings he included certain animals, like a cow and a lion, a lamb and a wolf, and a goat and a leopard. Though the animals have different facial expressions and body positions in each of Hicks' paintings, we see all the animals resting peacefully with each other. Hicks had a vision of a peaceful world, where natural enemies – like the lion and the lamb – could live in harmony. He believed, too, that all people were equals, and sometimes his animals in his paintings represented the vices and virtues of human beings. Hicks included both people and animals in his paintings.

Edward Hicks was born in Attleborough (now Langhorne), Pennsylvania, in 1780, four years after the American Revolution. Pennsylvania was founded by a Quaker hero, William Penn, who named the Quaker colony after his father. William Penn appears in Hicks' 1824 *Peaceable Kingdom* painting because of his important peace treaty with the Delaware Indians in 1682.

Hicks grew up on a farm of his Quaker cousins and always wanted to be a farmer, but when he was fourteen, he became an apprentice coachmaker and sign painter. He never had any formal art training or education, so Hicks is often referred to as a folk artist.

When Hicks was a young man, he was fond of drinking and fighting. At the age of twenty-two, he became seriously ill and almost died, and he believed his recovery was a sign from heaven. So Hicks changed his ways and joined the Society of Friends, becoming a wandering Quaker minister.

While Hicks devoted much of his energy promoting peace, love, and harmony, he had a violent temper and often doubted his own character. His group of

Peaceable Kingdom paintings often show us Hicks' struggle with himself. Many of Hick's most powerful paintings of the Peaceable Kingdom were painted when Hicks was troubled and uneasy. The animals in the Peaceable Kingdom paintings are crowded together and they look worried and afraid. Often the expressions on the animals' faces reflect the troubled feelings Edward Hicks, the artist, was experiencing. In one of Hicks' paintings, the lion has Hicks' face.

While the facial expressions and body positions of the animals and the children leading them vary, Hicks often used many restful shapes and curving lines in his paintings to portray peace and harmony as well. Hicks also included many visual echoes in his Peaceable Kingdom paintings, with shapes, colors and ideas repeating themselves on the canvas.

Hick's paintings always included two stories, one story showing us how life is, and how often troubled and painful Hicks was, and the other story showing us how beautiful the world can be, how humankind can live in harmony. These stories often paralled the Biblical and historical stories in the paintings as well.

Hicks died in 1849. He was a little known painter who also painted famous events from American history and the Bible, and Pennsylvania farm scenes. The last Peaceable Kingdom paintings Hicks produced seem to show us that Hicks was more at peace with himself in his old age. Those last paintings are serene and exude a quiet warmth and charming mystery.

EDWARD HICKS

VOCABULARY: canvas board, verse, peaceable kingdom, express, symbols, Quakers.

MATERIALS: watercolor, tempera or acrylic paint, brushes, posterboard or canvas board, or drawing supplies if you wish to draw instead of paint.

ACTIVITY:

1. Find and study at least two of Edward Hicks' paintings of *The Peaceable Kingdom*.

2. Like Edward Hicks, you will paint or draw your own peaceable kingdom.

3. Design your very own personal peaceable kingdom. Include people and/or symbols that you feel express peace for our world.

4. Like Mr. Hicks, you may want to write a poem or copy a verse and include it around your painting. The poem or verse should help describe your peaceable kingdom.

5. Be sure to sign your painting or drawing.

Evaluation   Name: _____

THINKING ABOUT EDWARD HICKS AND ME

Respond to four or more of the following questions/statements:

1. Describe and explain what symbols you chose for peace.

2. Compare the symbols – such as animals – that Edward Hicks used in his *Peaceable Kingdom* pictures to the symbols you used in your picture.

3. After studying one of Edward Hicks' Peaceable Kingdom paintings, what symbols do you think he would choose for peace if he were alive and painting today?

4. Write one or more ways that you can help create peace among your peers and among the members of your family.

5. Make a sketch of one of Hick's paintings on the back of this paper, or on a separate sheet. Then create and write a poem that you think would relate to this painting.

6. Write one or more paragraphs about what you have learned about this artist and/or what you have learned through your own creative project relating to this artist. Write this information on the opposite side of this sheet, or on a separate sheet of paper.

Winslow Homer
1836-1910

Winslow Homer was an American painter best known for his seascapes. During his painting career, in which he displayed his skill and mastery of sketching and watercolor, he often worked in his studio by the sea, whether it was in a remote fishing port – Tynemouth, England – on the North Sea, or in an isolated fishing village – Prouts Neck – on the coast of Maine. Winslow Homer became very adept at painting nature and showing us the frailty of men and women often at the mercy of nature's harsh elements.

Winslow Homer was born in Boston on February 24, 1836, to a very old New England family. He had a very happy childhood and his mother, who was an amateur painter, encouraged his artistic leanings. At the age of nineteen, Homer was apprenticed to the lithographic firm of John Bufford, and there he learned how to draw by copying other artists. Soon his own drawings were published in magazines such as *Ballou's Pictorial* and *Harper's Weekly*, and he began to work as a free-lance illustrator. In 1860, when he was twenty six, he had an exhibition of his paintings at the National Academy of Design in New York City.

During the Civil War, Homer became a pictorial reporter, drawing pictures for *Harper's* that showed everyday camp life, rather than battle scenes. He was a magazine illustrator until 1875. At this time in his life, he lived in New York City, but during the warm months, he liked to travel and go camping, hunting, fishing, and sketching.

In 1873, Homer began working with watercolor. Using watercolor enabled Homer to quickly put on paper his impressions of nature. As Homer matured as an artist, his oil paintings got larger and his concern for detail became more careful. He was also fond of painting many figures in isolation – figures all alone on canvas, whether it was a woman mending a fishing net, or a fisherman in his boat. Homer liked to spend a lot of time by himself, too; perhaps that is why his figures were more solitary. Homer spent his summers outdoors watercolor painting, capturing as much of nature and natural sunlight as possible.

When Homer was forty seven years old, the sea became the primary motif in his work. In many of his paintings, there is a sense of drama and suspense. There is also a strong narrative quality in his paintings which may be the result of his work as a journalist. In his oil painting *Fog Warning*, we see a lone fisherman in his dory (a boat with a narrow, flat bottom, and a high bow) trying to reach safety before the fog is too thick and the night too dark. In Homer's painting *The Gulf Stream*, we see a man lying motionless on the deck of a small sailboat. A hurricane has shredded the sails, sharks circle the boat, and a boat on the horizon passes by unseen and unseeing. We see the man in the boat is at the mercy of nature. In his painting *The Herring Net*, we see a group of men hunched over their catch. The distant ships are shrouded in mist and the dark sky and rolling waves warn of a brewing storm. Homer conveyed much suspense and mystery in his paintings and he is known for his mastery of dramatic concentration on the canvas, especially in his watercolor seascapes.

One of Homer's important contributions to American art was his mastery of watercolor. Prior to the nineteenth century, watercolor was used only for preliminary studies and sketches but Homer, like J.M.W. Turner, an English painter also adept at painting seascapes, used the medium for finished works.

In the late 1890s and early 1900s, Homer painted many brightly colored watercolor and pencil paintings depicting seascapes from Key West, the Bahamas, and Nassau. Winslow Homer painted continuously and adventurously until he died in his Prouts Neck studio on September 29, 1910.

Activity Sheet   Name: _____

WINSLOW HOMER

VOCABULARY: contrast, drama, suspense, mystery.

MATERIALS: paper, poster paints, watercolor paints, brushes, pencil.

ACTIVITY: Winslow Homer and Grandma Moses were both American painters. However, Homer's style was quite different from Grandma Moses'. Winslow Homer loved to paint mystery, drama, suspense and even danger in his scenes. He didn't paint familiar calm scenes like Grandma Moses.

1. Study some of the works of Winslow Homer and Grandma Moses.

2. You will imagine a scene with drama, mystery, suspense, and even danger, perhaps wo/man versus nature or wo/man verses animal.

3. First, draw the scene in pencil. Place the people and objects exactly where you want them.

4. Show good color contrast by placing light and dark colors next to each other. This gives a sense of drama.

5. Leave your audience in suspense. Don't let us know the outcome. Remember, you are the artist. You have control over your viewers. We can feel anything you wish us to feel; we can feel strong, angry, frightened, safe, or confused.

THINKING ABOUT WINSLOW HOMER AND ME

Respond to four or more of the following questions/statements:

1. Do you think artists have power over their viewers? Explain your answer.

2. Explain the differences between Homer's paintings and Grandma Moses' paintings. Which do you like better and why?

3. Homer's lifestyle was even different from Grandma Moses. With whose lifestyle do you identify?

4. Explain your painting. Describe the people or animals in it. Tell us what they are feeling or thinking. Tell us about the surroundings they are in.

5. What do you hope the audience will feel about your painting? Show your painting to your friends and family and write down their reactions.

6. Write one or more paragraphs about what you have learned about this artist and/or what you have learned through your own creative project relating to this artist. Write this information on the opposite side of this sheet, or on a separate sheet of paper.

Dorothea Lange
1895-1965

Dorothea Lange was a documentary photographer whose work had a profound impact on American history and the world of art. She recorded with her camera the beginning of the Great Depression, one of the darkest twentieth century events in America, and she is responsible for two of the most famous American photographs, *White Angel Bread Line* and *Migrant Mother*.

In *White Angel Bread Line*, she captures one of the greatest images of the Depression era. In the photo, we see an unshaven man who, like millions of other people during the Depression, probably had no money and no place to live. People like the man in the photo waited for hours in bread lines in order to get something to eat. We see in Lange's photograph the man leaning on a wooden railing, holding a tin cup between his forearms, his hands clenched together, and a grim look of despair on his face. The man in the photo is surrounded by many other men wearing hats, like himself, but the men's backs are facing the camera and we do not see their faces.

During the time of the Great Depression, which began in 1929, a series of droughts and dust storms occurred in the Midwest. Many farmers were unable to plant any crops as their land had been stripped of good soil. So many poor and hungry people left their farms for California, hoping to find work, food, and shelter. When these people arrived in California, there was nothing for them — no work, no food, no shelter. Because of this dire situation, the government had to react and they sent Lange to record the migrant workers' plight, where her pictures eventually helped them obtain food and shelter.

In her photograph *Migrant Mother*, Lange shows us the haggard and worn figure of a woman and her two children, the children's backs turned to the camera, resting their tousled heads on their mother's shoulders. The particular woman in Lange's photo, *Migrant Mother*, had no work as all the pea crops in Nipomo, California, where she was, had frozen. She and her children were living off frozen vegetables from the fields, and birds the children killed. These particular photographs — *White Angel Bread Line* and *Migrant Mother* — had a powerful impact on the conscience of American society and Lange's work established her as one of the greatest American photographers.

Dorothea Lange was born on May 26, 1895, in Hoboken, New Jersey. When she was seven years old, she contracted polio and her right leg became permanently damaged. Some mean school children often teased her and called her "Limpy." For the rest of her life, Lange walked with a limp.

After graduating from high school in 1913, Lange decided to make photography her life's work. She attended New York's Training School for Teachers for a short time before dropping out and apprenticing herself to Arnold Genthe, the photographer of San Francisco's 1906 earthquake. In 1917, Lange took a photography course from Clarence White (who also taught another photographer, Margaret Bourke-White), and a year later she opened up a portrait studio in San Francisco.

Lange was quite successful as a portrait photographer. She took many pictures of people and charged them very high prices. But after awhile, she realized she wanted to photograph all kinds of people, even those who could not afford to pay her. She was very much interested and concerned with the plight of those in difficult and trying situations.

In 1920, she married an artist named Maynard Dixon, and traveled with him, photographing the poverty, joblessness, and helplessness on Arizona's ranches and reservations. They had two sons and because Lange's work frequently took her far from home, she often had to "board out" her children, paying other families to care for her sons. Lange married again in 1935 and with her second husband, Paul Taylor, a social scientist, they teamed together, documenting poverty in rural America.

Dorothea Lange was a simple, direct, honest, and friendly woman whose photographs of the Japanese internment camps in Wyoming, the migrant workers in California, and the Great Depression vividly recorded the images of thousands of people. She worked for *Life* magazine in the 1950s and many of her photographs appeared on its covers. She was one of eight women photographers in New York City's Museum of Modern Art exhibit presented and organized by another famous photographer, Edward Steichen. In 1964, the same year she completed a book of photos on the American country woman, she was asked to have a one woman show at the Museum of Modern Art. She was, at that time, only one of six photographers ever to have presented a one person exhibit.

Dorothea Lange died on October 11, 1965, after battling cancer of the esophagus. After her death, a photographic study of her children and grandchildren was published in 1973. It was entitled *To A Cabin*. Because of Lange's dedication and artistry, we are fortunate to be left with a vast, rich legacy of her moving and quietly brilliant photographs, many highlighting and defining the current social dilemmas plaguing our society.

DOROTHEA LANGE

VOCABULARY: Great Depression, socially conscious, droughts, social problems, plight.

MATERIALS: interesting colored photos, or black and white photos from magazines or newspaper, a sheet of 9 x 12 white construction paper, scissors, glue.

ACTIVITY:

1. Study about some of Dorothea Lange's work.

2. Dorothea Lange's art was photography and through her art she recorded history. She portrayed the poor and homeless people during the Great Depression and during the droughts of the Midwest.

3. Like Dorothea Lange, you will compose a photograph that has a socially conscious theme which shows your viewers someone's or something's plight. For example, your composition might show us an oil spill, the destruction of a rain forest, or a homeless person.

4. Select photographs from magazines and newspapers and arrange them together with glue on a sheet of construction paper. The collage will become your photograph.

5. The more you are aware of a problem situation, the better you may be equipped in understanding and solving it. As you compose your photo collage, try to think of solutions to the problem(s) that your collage is about.

Evaluation   Name: _____

THINKING ABOUT DOROTHEA LANGE AND ME

Respond to four or more of the following questions/statements:

1. One of the purposes of art is to communicate a message. Describe the message you tried to communicate with your photography collage.

2. Explain why it is sometimes very important to portray a theme that may not be pretty or pleasant.

3. It is said that a "picture is worth a thousand words." Write a story on a separate sheet of paper about one of Dorothea Lange's photographs.

4. Why do you think Dorothea Lange chose to be a socially conscious photographer?

5. Look closely at a children's book that has photographs rather than illustrations in it. Write why you think the author or publisher chose to use photographs instead of illustrations in this book.

6. Write one or more paragraphs about what you have learned about this artist and/or what you have learned through your own creative project relating to this artist. Write this information on the opposite side of this sheet, or on a separate sheet of paper.

Henri Matisse
(ahn REE mah TEES)
1869-1954

In Le Cateau-Cambrésis, France, on December 31, 1869, a baby boy was born to a grain merchant and his wife. This boy, Henri Matisse, grew up to become one of the finest and most famous artists in the world. Matisse organized the colors in his painting, and later in his collages, like no one else before him. He was an artist in love with joyous, vibrant color, color in musical harmony with the lines, shapes, and patterns on his canvas.

Henri Matisse was eighteen years old when he moved from Le Cateau-Cambrésis to Paris to study law. After earning his law degree there, Matisse began taking formal art lessons. One of his first art teachers was Gustave Moreau, a very well-known and important artist and teacher. Matisse worked very hard in his lessons. He had a formal academic art education and he learned the style and techniques of the old masters of art, such as Raphael, by copying over twenty famous paintings. Matisse made sculptures, too, and he studied the work of Rodin, a famous French sculptor. Matisse also studied the theories and techniques of the Impressionists, like Monet and Manet, who were painting in France at the time.

Matisse spent almost an entire year in 1898, in the south of France, painting, where the clear light and color of the landscape near the Mediterranean Sea influenced his work. Years later, in 1906 and again in 1912, Matisse traveled to Tangiers, Morocco, to study, and once there, fell in love with the light and surrounding landscape. He later painted many beautiful reclining odalisques, women who were sometimes slaves in a harem, reclining against pillows, wearing colorful jewelry and wide, loose pants. Matisse is sometimes called an Orientalist, a term used to describe European painters who painted figures and landscapes influenced by their journeys to North Africa — where Morocco is — and the Near East.

By 1900, Matisse was the leader of the Post-Impressionists, those painters working after the Impressionist painters. Matisse was known as an "Expressionist." Other artists like van Gogh, Cézanne, and Gauguin were also part of this art movement called "Expressionism." Matisse and other Expressionists painted their emotional reactions to the community around them. These painters were known for their radical style: they experimented with bright, bold colors in ways that had not ever been seen before.

In 1905, a group of painters had a showing of their paintings at the Salon D'Automne in Paris. An art critic who saw the paintings there thought they were the works of wild beasts, hence, Matisse and the other artists exhibiting became known as the "Fauvism," (which in French means "wild beasts.") Matisse was known as the leader of "Fauves," too. His painting, *The Joy of Life*, painted in 1905-1906, shows and defines for us the spirit of Fauvism. In the painting, there are many simply drawn figures dancing, playing musical instruments, and enjoying one another's company.

Matisse's wife, Amelie Payayre, a hat maker, and his two sons and daughter, Marguerite, often modeled for him. Matisse painted many landscapes and flowers, but it was the human figure that Matisse enjoyed painting the most.

When Matisse was old and ill and confined to bed, he began making paper cut-outs. Since he was crippled, it was easier for him to cut-out interesting shapes from paper than it was to paint on canvas. The paper shapes he cut out – flowers, leaves, shells – were called "positives," and the paper cut-aways (the leftover paper scraps) were called "negatives." He used both in his collages.

One of the last projects Matisse worked on was a religious commission. He devoted his time from 1948 through 1952 creating the Chapel of the Dominicans at Vence, France. He designed everything in the chapel from the stained glass windows to the vestments that the priest wore. He wanted to create a church full of joy and peace.

Matisse loved to create and it was his work that made him most happy. He believed that the purpose of pictures was to give pleasure. Through his use of jewel-like colors and simple, bold lines, Matisse gives the viewers of his art infinite pleasure and peace.

Name _____

HENRI MATISSE

VOCABULARY: collage, rhythmic, organic, design, inspire.

MATERIALS: construction paper or multi-colored paper, glue, scissors, (posterboard is optional).

ACTIVITY:

1. Find and study some of the works of Henri Matisse.

2. You will arrange a rhythmic and colorful collage similar to one that Matisse might have made.

3. Fold your paper in halves or quarters and cut out different shapes. Create new shapes and designs. Cut out as many shapes as you want.

4. Examine your shapes. Try to arrange them in the most interesting way you can imagine. Once you have decided on the order of the shapes, glue them down on a piece of paper or on a piece of posterboard.

5. Write a story or a poem about your completed collage.

Evaluation   Name _____

THINKING ABOUT MATISSE AND ME

Respond to four or more of the following questions/statements:

1. What did you wonder about as you were arranging your collage?

2. Are you pleased with the completed collage? Explain:

3. Pretend that you cannot see. Feel your shapes and describe your collage below.

4. Pretend that your collage is going to be sold through a museum catalog. Write a title for your collage and write a description of it for a museum catalog.

5. Why do you think Matisse enjoyed making collages? Will you make other collages on your own? Why?

6. Write one or more paragraphs about what you have learned about this artist and/or what you have learned through your own creative project relating to this artist. Write this information on the opposite side of this sheet, or on a separate sheet of paper.

Claude Monet
(moNAY or mawNEH)
1840-1926

Claude Monet was a French painter who became the leading member of the Impressionists. He was born in Paris on November 14, 1840, though he moved with his family to LeHavre when he was five. Monet knew early in life that he wanted to become a painter, although his parents discouraged his aspirations and wanted him instead to work in their grocery store. Monet's aunt, who had been a painter as well, gave Monet money to study art in Paris when he was nineteen years old.

In 1870, Monet married his Parisian girlfriend, Camille, who appeared in many of his paintings, and eventually they had two dark-haired sons, Jean and Michel. Monet and Camille were very poor but they had two wealthy friends, Alice and Ernest Hochedé, who had money to buy Monet's paintings for their summer palace. When Ernest Hochedé's department stores went bankrupt, Ernest was humiliated and he left his pregnant wife and five children, and fled the country. Because Monet and Camille were good friends of Alice, they all decided to share a house together. There were eight children in the house: Monet and Camille's two sons, and Alice's six children, four girls and two boys. Soon after, unfortunately, Camille died from tuberculosis, and Alice was left to care for all of the children while Monet tried to paint.

Several years later, Monet moved the family to a big, pink house in Giverny, a village near Vernon. The sky, water, reflections, trees, and flowers in the garden at Giverny gave Monet much artistic challenge. It was at Giverny that Monet painted his most famous flower paintings, the water lilies on his pond.

It wasn't until Monet had sold many paintings that he was able to finally afford to buy the house in Giverny. He was fifty years old. Shortly afterwards, Ernest Hochedé, Alice's husband, died, and a year after that, Alice and Monet were married.

Monet's step-daughter, Blanche, who also painted, helped him carry many of his painting supplies around their large garden, and Monet portrayed some of his children in his paintings, including Blanche and her two sisters, as they fished from a boat in the River Epte.

Monet was seldom satisfied with his paintings and he was constantly reworking them. Sometimes, if he was unhappy with his paintings, he would burn them.

Monet was considered a leader of the Impressionist movement. Impressionism is a style of painting characterized by short brush strokes and patches of bright colors. This was a style of painting first introduced by Edouard Manet, another French painter living at the same time as Monet. Many art critics, along with the public, hostilely viewed Impressionism as revolutionary. When an art critic saw Monet's painting, *Impression: Sunrise*, exhibited in 1874, he defined the show as "impressionist." Much of the public did not like Monet's "impressions" of subjects. People were used to seeing realistic paintings, with defined shapes and dark colors, that told a story. They thought Monet's painting – of his impression of sunlight reflected in the water – looked unfinished.

While he painted many things from steam engines to cathedrals to haystacks, Monet was always concerned with the effects of outdoor light and atmosphere; he was also one of the first to paint landscapes entirely out of doors. He even scheduled lunch with his family at 11:30 nearly every day so that he could take advantage of the afternoon light. Monet is most famous for his garden scenes, his series of Japanese footbridges, and, of course, his water lily paintings which he painted towards the end of his life.

In Paris, the Musee D'Orsay houses one of the largest collections of Impressionist paintings. Monet's mural-sized water lily paintings are at the Orangerie (the King's greenhouse) in the Tuileries Gardens.

As Monet became older, he developed cataracts on his eyes and almost became blind. When he could barely see, he continued to paint, and his paintings were primarily red. It was only until a doctor operated on Monet's eyes that all the other colors returned to his paintings.

In 1926, the year Monet finished his water lily paintings, he died at the age of eighty six, a man of revolutionary vision who painted what he saw. His way of seeing and of painting had an enormous impact and influence on his fellow artists and successors.

Activity Sheet   Name _____

CLAUDE MONET

VOCABULARY: footbridge, recreate, mural, Impressionism, reflection.

MATERIALS: crayons, colored pencils, colored chalk, and/or tempera paints, and paper.

ACTIVITY:

1. Study some of the works of Claude Monet, including the gardens and the bridges in the gardens.

2. Design your own footbridge and garden on a sheet of paper. Make your own Impressionist painting of a garden.

Evaluation   Name _____

THINKING ABOUT MONET AND ME

Respond to four or more of the following questions/statements:

1. Why do you think Monet enjoyed painting nature and outdoor scenes?

2. What kind of scenes do you like to paint? Explain:

3. Why do you think that Monet painted the same subjects over and over again?

4. How is your painting similar to and how is it different from a bridge scene that Monet painted?

5. What did you think about as you were creating the footbridge scene?

6. Write one or more paragraphs about what you have learned about this artist and/or what you have learned through your own creative project relating to this artist. Write this information on the opposite side of this sheet, or on a separate sheet of paper.

Henry Moore
1898-1986

Henry Moore was an English sculptor whose bronze, marble, stone, or wood sculptures were famous for their monumental simplicity. Many of Moore's sculptures look as if they have been shaped by natural forces and a lot of these sculptures were specifically designed for permanent display outdoors. Moore is famous for his series of reclining women though he also did male figures, mother and child groups, and masks and heads, carved from stone. In addition to his sculptures, Moore did many drawings, particularly of Londoners in underground shelters during World War II. He also did many drawings of coal miners at work, visiting the colliery (a coal mine) where his father had worked.

Henry Moore was born into a coal-mining family in Castleford, a small coal-mining town near Leeds in the north of England. He was the seventh child of Raymond Spencer Moore and Mary Baker. Throughout his entire lifetime and career, Moore remained a simple and honest man very proud of his working-class origins and ancestors.

From 1909-1915, Moore attended the Castleford Grammar School where he had won a scholarship. He had a very good art teacher there, Alice Gostick, who greatly encouraged and helped Moore in his pursuit of art. Moore already knew he wanted to become a sculptor but his father wanted him to be trained as a schoolteacher, like his older brother and sisters.

Moore did teach at his old primary school for a short while before joining the British Army where he was stationed in France. After his stint in the Army, he resumed teaching and then went to the Leeds School of Art for two years. Moore spent much of his time there studying drawing, though he still had a strong desire to be a sculptor. At the end of his second year at Leeds, he passed the sculpture examination and was awarded a scholarship to study at the Royal College of Art in London. Attending the Royal College was important to Moore because he was able to study sculpture for three years. But it was equally important to him to be living in London where all the museums — particularly the British Museum — gave him many opportunities to study the displays of sculpture. He was very much inspired by ancient Mexican and African stone carvings and he found the stark beauty, power, and depth within them very magnetic.

In 1928, Moore had his first one-man exhibition at the Warren Gallery in London, and he also began his first public commission, a relief carving on the London Transport Board headquarters building. A year later, Moore married

Irina Radetsky, a painting student at the Royal College of Art. In 1931, Moore had a one-man exhibition in the Leicester Galleries in London where his abstract sculptures received a lot of negative criticism from the press. Because of this harsh criticism, Moore was asked to resign his position at the Royal College of Art and in 1932, he left to start a sculpture department at the Chelsea School of Art.

Henry Moore's massive sculptures often looked as if they were produced through the wearing away of stone by the wind and waters of time. His sculptures were abstract and subtle with smooth, graceful lines. Because his sculptures didn't look as if they were carved with human tools, composed as they were of flowing convex (flowing outward) and concave (flowing inward) forms, they harmoniously blended very well with natural environments.

Moore used holes or openings in his work to emphasize its three-dimensional quality. The space his actual form took was referred to as "positive space," while the holes or space left in the form was referred to as "negative space."

Moore died at the age of eighty eight, a very much honored and celebrated artist. A few of his major commissions are the sculptures for UNESCO headquarters in Paris (1957-58), for the Lincoln Center in New York City (1963-65), and for the East Building of the National Gallery of Art in Washington, D.C. (1978).

Name _____

HENRY MOORE

VOCABULARY: positive space, negative space, mass, simplified, gallery.

MATERIALS: modeling clay (oil based), plastic knife, clear plastic container.

ACTIVITY:

1. Find and study photographs of Henry Moore's sculptures.

2. Like Henry Moore, you will create a sculpture with a simplified form. Perhaps you'll sculpt a human or an animal form.

3. When you have chosen what you will sculpt, use the plastic knife to cut the clay and use your hands to roll it.

4. Examine the possibilities of form. Think about the positive space (the form itself) and the negative space (the holes in the form).

5. After you have finished your sculpture, put it under a clear plastic container to represent a famous sculpture in an art gallery.

Evaluation   Name _____

THINKING ABOUT HENRY MOORE AND ME

Respond to four or more of the following questions/statements:

1. Which do you think is more important and which do you think is more interesting: positive space or negative space? Explain:

2. Describe your sculpted form to someone who isn't able to see it.

3. Imagine that the sculpture you made is very large. Make a list of places where this sculpture could be displayed, such as in or near a city park.

4. If you were a professional sculptor, what kind of sculptures would you like to sculpt? Explain:

5. List the titles of at least six of your favorite sculptures that were done by other artists.

6. Write one or more paragraphs about what you have learned about this artist and/or what you have learned through your own creative project relating to this artist. Write this information on the opposite side of this sheet, or on a separate sheet of paper.

T.S. Denison & Co., Inc.   56   *Let's Meet Famous Artists*

Anna Mary Robertson Moses
(Grandma Moses)
1860-1961

When Anna Mary Robertson was a young girl, her brothers and sisters called her Sissy. And when Anna Mary Robertson became older, the world knew her as Grandma Moses. Grandma Moses did not begin painting seriously until she was almost eighty years old, but until she was one hundred and one, she painted eagerly and continuously. Grandma Moses was called a folk artist or primitive painter. Both those titles mean that the artist never had any art lessons or formal training in painting. Grandma Moses became internationally famous for documenting rural life in the late nineteenth and early twentieth centuries. She painted the surrounding countryside of her childhood farm and painted scenes showing us the changing seasons, her schoolhouse, cutting a Christmas tree, catching a Thanksgiving turkey, and collecting sap from maple trees to make syrup.

Anna Mary was born on a farm in Greenwich, New York, on September 7, 1860, just as the United States was entering the Civil War. All ten Robertson children had work to do on the farm. There were eggs to gather from the hen house, cows to milk, weeds to pull from the vegetable garden, and wood to carry for the kitchen stove. But after all their chores were done, the children enjoyed playing outdoors, skating and sledding, going to county fairs, and picking cherries in the orchard. Anna Mary fondly remembered all these happy days from her childhood and much later, recalled these days in her paintings.

Anna Mary's father was something of a painter, too, once painting and decorating the walls of their house with pretty scenes. Anna Mary's father liked beautiful things and he encouraged his children to draw. Anna Mary loved color and because she had no paints, she used grape juice and crushed berries for color, or carpenter's blue chalk or the red dye her father used to mark their sheep.

When Anna Mary was twelve, she left the family farm to earn her living as a hired girl. After working many years for several different families, Anna Mary went to work for a family named James when she was twenty six years old. Also working for the family at this time as a hired man was a young farmer named Thomas Moses. It wasn't long before Anna Mary and Thomas fell in love and became engaged. They were married in Hoosick Falls, a town not far from the farm where Anna Mary was born, and after their wedding ceremony, they departed for Virginia, where they rented a farm in the town of Staunton. During this time of her life, Anna Mary had no time to paint. There was much work to do on the farm and the house, and there were many children to love and raise as well. When her children grew up and moved away, Anna Mary began painting again. Her first large picture was a painted fireboard, a screen used to cover the fireplace. She used a big brush – a brush she had used to paint the floor – to paint a lake scene on the fireboard.

After her husband, Thomas, died in 1927, Anna Mary began to create worsted embroidery pictures at the urging of her daughter. Anna Mary gave away as gifts many of the embroidered pictures of landscapes made out of worsted yarn, but when arthritis made it too difficult to continue the needlework, Anna Mary turned to painting.

Grandma Moses found inspiration for her paintings in the pictures on greeting cards and calendars. She also liked the New England farm scenes depicted on the Currier and Ives prints. When Grandma Moses had done quite a few paintings, her son and daughter-in-law- took them to the W. D. Thomas Pharmacy in Hoosick Falls where there was a women's exchange for local women to display and sell things they'd made.

One day an art collector from New York City named Louis J. Caldor glanced in the Thomas drugstore window and saw Grandma Moses' paintings. He liked the paintings very much and bought the paintings in the drugstore. He even wanted more paintings by Grandma Moses! Louis Caldor gave Grandma Moses a lot of encouragement and when he returned to New York City, he took her paintings and showed them to many art galleries. Eventually, the paintings were shown in the Museum of Modern Art in New York. Then Mr. Caldor showed Grandma Moses' paintings to a well known art dealer and gallery owner. This gallery owner's name was Otto Kallir and he was very interested in American folk art. He offered to give Grandma Moses a show in his gallery, the Galerie St. Etienne.

When the exhibit, called "What a Farmwife Painted," opened in 1940, Grandma Moses was eighty years old. After this showing, Grandma Moses soon became very famous and she won many awards for her art. She was even presented an award from Harry Truman, the President of the United States at the time. One of her paintings, entitled *July Fourth*, hangs in the White House. Grandma Moses worked very hard, satisfying all the museums and art collectors who wanted her paintings. She painted twenty six more pictures after her one hundredth birthday and when she was almost one hundred and one, she had to go into a nursing home in Hoosick Falls, where she could rest and be taken care of. She didn't like it there at all and she could not paint, and she wanted to return to her farm in Eagle Bridge.

Grandma Moses died in the nursing home on December 13, 1961, leaving behind many cheerful paintings recalling her childhood and many enthusiastic admirers of her work.

Name _____

ANNA MARY ROBERTSON MOSES
Grandma Moses

VOCABULARY: folk artist, landscape painting, scene, rural, detail.

MATERIALS: reference books, paper, poster paints, watercolor paints, brushes, pencil.

ACTIVITY: Like Grandma Moses, you will illustrate a scene that is familiar to you and your family. Perhaps you will paint your family celebrating a holiday, sharing a meal, working together, or playing together.

1. First draw the scene in pencil. Place the people and objects exactly where you want them.

2. If you are doing a landscape painting, you may want to look outside or paint outside to see the trees, clouds, and all of the colors.

3. If you are painting an indoor scene, look at the room you are painting. Grandma Moses painted in detail, so you may also want to add certain colors and patterns in the rug, floor, furniture, and walls.

4. Choose a scene you like and one that is familiar to you. You will be very happy with your painting if it reminds you of good times.

Evaluation   Name _____

THINKING ABOUT ANNA MARY ROBERTSON MOSES AND ME
Grandma Moses

Respond to four or more of the following questions/statements:

1. Describe any people you know who are elderly and who do some interesting activities.

2. Let's pretend you are much older than your parents are now. Explain what you think you would be doing for enjoyment.

3. Why do you think people like things that are familiar to them? Explain:

4. Describe at least two differences between a rural landscape and a city landscape.

5. Describe two or more scenes that you would like to paint.

6. Write one or more paragraphs about what you have learned about this artist and/or what you have learned through your own creative project relating to this artist. Write this information on the opposite side of this sheet, or on a separate sheet of paper.

Georgia O'Keeffe
1887-1986

As a child, Georgia Totto O'Keeffe, the second of seven children, was very observant and very independent. She was aware of every detail surrounding her and her memory for recalling special events and details was very remarkable. Her sensitive awareness of her surroundings helped her become a very fine artist who is famous now for her large, beautiful oil and watercolor paintings of flowers and landscapes.

Georgia Totto O'Keeffe was born in 1887 on a farm in Sun Prairie, Wisconsin. She was named after her mother's father, George Totto. When she was ten years old, she and her sisters took painting lessons. By the time she was thirteen, she knew in her heart that she wanted to be an artist.

O'Keeffe had many art lessons throughout high school but she had several critical teachers who discouraged her. They wanted her to paint what *they* saw, rather than what *she* saw. She was disappointed with this instruction but she worked hard and stuck to what she believed was right for her. She did not like to draw what others had drawn. Her vision of art was original and imaginative.

At eighteen, O'Keeffe studied at The Art Institute of Chicago and then later at the Art Students League in New York. She wanted to paint what was important to her, but she still had teachers who thought she should study painting by imitating the works of others. She wanted to continue her studies in New York City, but because of financial difficulties, she had to return to Chicago to live with her relatives. While O'Keeffe was there, she got the measles (which weakened her eyesight temporarily). Then she left to join her family who were now living in Virginia.

At the University of Virginia, O'Keeffe studied painting under Alon Bemont and for the first time, she felt secure under someone else's teaching. Bemont greatly influenced O'Keeffe. He felt it was a painter's most important duty to fill space in a beautiful way. O'Keeffe agreed with this thinking.

O'Keeffe very much wanted to study under Arthur Wesley Dow, Alon Bemont's former teacher, in New York City. But in order to study with him and take his classes, O'Keeffe had to save her money. So she worked for two years in Amarillo, Texas, as the supervisor of art for the public schools. She enjoyed the landscapes of Texas very much, and the plains, ocean, and sunsets there would later play an important part in her painting. She returned to Texas several years later to teach in Canyon, and while also working at her art, she tried to simplify her creations and get to the essence of what she wanted the painting to say.

In 1914, O'Keeffe returned to New York City to study with Dow, and she gained new insight and inspiration for her work. In 1915, she went to South Carolina to teach, and while there, she sent several of her drawings to her old school friend for comments. O'Keeffe's friend sent her drawings, without her knowledge, to a very important and well-known photographer, Alfred Stieglitz, who owned an art gallery called "291." Alfred Stieglitz was a powerful figure in the New York City art world and he liked O'Keeffe's drawings right away, soon displaying them in his gallery.

Thus began a very close relationship between Stieglitz and O'Keeffe. As artists, they supported each other's work and drew from each other much inspiration. In 1924, Stieglitz and O'Keeffe were married. Stieglitz took many beautiful and unusual photographs of O'Keeffe during their long relationship. Some photographs show us only O'Keeffe's hands or neck or back. The photographs are very simple, stark and sensual, much like O'Keeffe's paintings.

Almost from her very first exhibition, O'Keeffe had success as a painter. During the period from 1916-1919, her work was very abstract. As her own personal vision of art became more defined, her paintings turned more toward reality, and she produced many still lifes, landscapes, and flower paintings in the Cubist-Realist style. She portrayed the world simply as she saw it and her vision had many unusual perspectives. Flowers were her favorite subjects and she would sometimes paint flowers very close-up or very far away, or sometimes she would only show us a part of her subject on the canvas. She gave us this new perspective because she wanted to make us look at the beauty of flowers in a new light. O'Keeffe painted very popular and monumental paintings of Oriental poppies, calla lilies, larkspurs, hollyhocks, petunias, and morning glories. In over nine hundred paintings, watercolors, and drawings, she created art that was innovative and influential in a style that was clearly powerful and sensual.

In 1929, O'Keeffe first visited New Mexico and loved the new landscapes that greeted her. She traveled to New Mexico almost every summer to work and was inspired by the natural imagery of the Southwest, painting stories of feathers, bones, and the desert. After Stieglitz died in 1946, O'Keeffe settled in Taos, New Mexico, permanently, living in the desert and painting there until she was almost blind. Georgia O'Keeffe was still working at her art until her death at age ninety eight.

Name _____

GEORGIA O'KEEFFE

VOCABULARY: detail, signature, still life, close-up.

MATERIALS: flowers (or a picture of a real flower), heavy paper such as posterboard, brushes, pencil, tempera paint or watercolors, pencil and paper for observation notes.

ACTIVITY:

1. Study photographs of Georgia O'Keeffe's paintings of flowers.

2. Like Georgia O'Keeffe, you'll paint a still life painting of a flower.

3. Observe a flower for five or more minutes. Write down your observations of the flower.

4. Paint a close-up of the flower.

5. Sign your painting with your special signature.

Evaluation   Name _____

THINKING ABOUT GEORGIA O'KEEFFE AND ME

Respond to four or more of the following questions/statements:

1. Did your still life painting of a flower close-up remind you of another object(s)? Explain:

2. What kind of flower did you paint? What did you wonder about as you painted your flower?

3. Do you think it was in character for Georgia O'Keeffe to paint such big close-up paintings? Why or why not?

4. If you could go anywhere to paint, where would you go? Why?

5. Georgia O'Keeffe loved to paint the skulls of animals. Do you think they make good painting subjects? Explain:

6. Write one or more paragraphs about what you have learned about this artist and/or what you have learned through your own creative project relating to this artist. Write this information on the opposite side of this sheet, or on a separate sheet of paper.

Jackson Pollock
(PAHL uhk)
1912-1956

Jackson Pollock, an American painter, loved painting on huge canvases so that he had the freedom of movement to use his entire body when he painted. Jackson Pollock was the leading innovator of the technique known as Action Painting. Pollock poured and splattered colors on the canvas, rather than applying the paint with a brush. He felt that Action Painting allowed the artist, rather than the brush, to be the primary source of energy shaping and controlling the paint and the process of painting. One of Pollock's huge paintings, entitled *One*, is eight feet ten inches in height and seventeen feet five and one half inches in length. The painting is rich and alive with color and it's hanging in the Museum of Modern Art in New York City.

Jackson Pollock was born in Cody, Wyoming, on January 28, 1912, but he was raised in California and Arizona. He studied painting in Los Angeles and was introduced to the art movement known as Surrealism. When he was eighteen years old, he followed a brother to New York City, and he enrolled at the Art Students League under his brother's teacher, Thomas Hart Benton. Through the years of the Great Depression, when the United States was experiencing an economic crisis, Pollock was able to support himself as an easel painter and in 1943, he had his first one-man show at Peggy Guggenheim's Art of This Century Gallery in New York City. After his first one-man show, Pollock continued to have new exhibits of his work nearly every year.

Pollock's work went through a number of transitions. When he worked under Thomas Hart Benton, he did a number of small landscapes. Then his painting became more abstract and displayed the influence of the modern Spanish painters Pablo Picasso and Joan Miró. His work was also influenced by the theories of the Surrealists, those artists whose imagery in their work was very dreamlike and unreal.

In the 1940s, Pollock wanted to find a way to include his entire personality in his painting and in 1947, he first experimented with poured painting. He discovered that this technique gave his mural-size canvases areas of innovative and complex linear patterns. For awhile, in 1951 and 1952, he painted almost only in black and white, but then he returned to color again.

Jackson Pollock was an abstract painter, a painter who expressed his feelings on the canvas in seemingly random patterns and shapes. Abstract paintings do not show us realistic pictures but rather, they show us unique and inventive mixtures of a variety of lines, shapes, and colors. One of the most important contributions to the twentieth century art world is the invention of abstract painting.

Pollock, like Vincent van Gogh, believed that since the invention of photography, one need not paint realistically any more. So both Pollock and van Gogh altered their painting procedures, van Gogh making his paintings very rough in texture so that they would be as different as possible from photographs, and Pollock utilizing Action Painting, painting not only with his arms, but with the motion of his entire body.

Pollock's health slowly deteriorated and so his production of work slowed down. Some of his important paintings done in the last few years of his life are *White Light* and *Scent* and *Blue Poles: Number II*, one of his most famous abstract paintings, completed in 1952. Jackson Pollock died in a car accident on August 11, 1956, in East Hampton, New York. His important contribution to the twentieth century art world, however, remains. Pollock was an artist who believed a can of paint was a storehouse of creative forces ready for him to pour or splatter onto canvas. His revolutionary technique encouraged other artists to experiment with their process and materials as well.

JACKSON POLLOCK

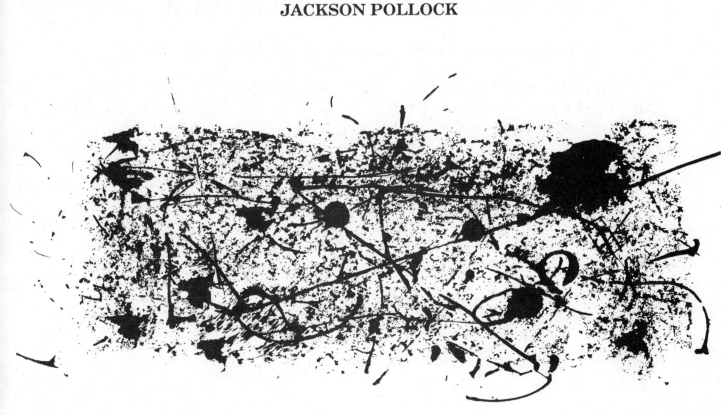

VOCABULARY: Action Painting, emotional release, motion.

MATERIALS: a smock or large old men's shirt, roll of inexpensive news-print paper, wide brushes or sponge brushes, coffee cans, watered down tempera paints.

ACTIVITY:

1. Study photographs of Jackson Pollock's paintings.

2. As a class, go outside wearing smocks. Each person gets one can of watered down tempera paint and a brush. Line up along one side of the newsprint paper that is lying on the ground. At your teacher's command, begin your Action Painting.

3. As an individual, go outside wearing your smock. Lay your newsprint paper on the grass or cement. Have newspaper underneath to prevent a mess. Begin your Action Painting.

Name _____

THINKING ABOUT JACKSON POLLOCK AND ME

Respond to four or more of the following questions/statements:

1. Compared to the other styles of painting you have done, how do you feel about Mr. Pollock's style of painting? Explain:

2. As you were doing the Action Painting exercise, describe the emotions you felt.

3. Pretend you are Jackson Pollock. Tell in your own words why you do Action Painting.

4. Pick any of the artists you have studied so far. Whose style is similar to and different from Jackson Pollock's style?

5. Let's pretend Mr. Pollock's paints could talk. What do you think they would say as they were being flung at the canvas? What would the paints say once they were settled on the canvas?

6. Write one or more paragraphs about what you have learned about this artist and/or what you have learned through your own creative project relating to this artist. Write this information on the opposite side of this sheet, or on a separate sheet of paper.

Rembrandt
(RHEM brant)
1606-1669

Harmenszoon van Rijn Rembrandt was a Dutch painter famous for his portraits and for his skilled mastery at depicting light and shadow in his paintings. In Rembrandt's portraits, we often see the subject's face half shaded. The darker, more obscured half of the face might suggest to us the inner secrets, dreams, and ambitions of that person. The other side of the subject's face is often clearly shown, in full, bright, light, and this may be a view of the person as he or she would like to be seen. In Rembrandt's day, in the seventeenth century, there were no cameras or photographers, so many people commissioned artists to paint their likeness on canvas. Rembrandt was one of the most popular artists of his time, and many people who could afford to have their portraits painted chose Rembrandt to portray them.

Harmenszoon van Rijn Rembrandt was born on July 15, 1606, in Leiden, Holland, the eighth of nine children. Rembrandt's father was a miller who ground wheat into fine flour for bread, and his mother was the daughter of a baker. Rembrandt began studying painting when he was fifteen years old, and by the time he was twenty three, he was already regarded as a master painter. Rembrandt painted many landscape paintings and paintings depicting scenes from the Bible. He painted over four hundred portraits and painted many portraits of his family and friends and of himself. He painted his father, Harmen, wearing a feathered hat and a velvet robe. One of Rembrandt's most famous paintings, *The Syndics at the Drapers' Guild*, now at the Rijksmuseum in Amsterdam, shows us a group of black-robed men, looking towards us as if we have interrupted their meeting. Rembrandt was very skilled at suggesting action in a still picture. Another famous painting of his – *The Feast of Belshazzar* – shows us a very surprised looking turbanned king. The king's group of friends also looked surprised, so surprised that two glasses of wine are knocked over. We can see wine spilling from the glasses and we can almost imagine the sort of shock and surprise Belshazzar and his friends are experiencing from their spilled wine. This painting is hanging in the National Gallery in London.

In 1634, Rembrandt married Saskia van Uylenburgh, the daughter of a wealthy burgomaster. Together they had a son named Titus. When Saskia died, after having been sick for a long time, Rembrandt was extremely sad. He continued painting, however, and his sadness over his wife's death seemed to bring to his portraits solemn and contemplative qualities. Rembrandt later fell in love again with a women, Hendrickje Stoffels, who had moved to Rembrandt's house to care for Titus. Rembrandt and Hendrickje had a daughter named

Cornelia. Rembrandt painted portraits of both Saskia and Hendrickje, the mothers of his children. In his portrait of his beautiful wife, Saskia, we see her dressed in a sumptuous velvet gown and feathered hat, and she is wearing many jewels. In one of his later portraits of Hendrickje, painted in 1662, Rembrandt has portrayed her as Venus, holding and caressing the face of a winged Cupid.

Because Rembrandt was such a successful and popular artist, he had many requests from people to do paintings for them. Rembrandt became very wealthy, and he enjoyed spending all his money on fine clothes, jewelry, art objects, and beautiful furniture for his fine house. He liked to use many of these precious jewels and art ornaments in his paintings, and he liked dressing his subjects (and himself) in costly furs and fabrics. He was able to reproduce in minute detail every facet of a jewel, or every plush fold of a cape. Rembrandt's spending habits got him into a bit of trouble, though, and he eventually had to declare bankruptcy. After this, Hendrickje and his son, Titus, managed his financial affairs. They also helped support the family by opening a shop for the sale of Rembrandt's paintings and prints.

Rembrandt was a very prolific artist, creating over six hundred paintings, over a thousand drawings, and almost three hundred etchings. He worked very carefully and slowly, though, and his sittings for each portrait were often done over a two or three month period. After the paint dried on a particular painting, he would go over the surface of the canvas again, using larger or smaller brushstrokes until the paint built up to the thickness of half a finger.

Rembrandt died at the age of sixty three, on October 4, 1669, in Amsterdam. After his death, his popularity as a painter continued to rise. Rembrandt is now considered a giant in the history of art, and his portraits are considered masterpieces of light and shadow, communicating to us the quiet wisdom and inner strength of its subjects.

HARMENSZOON VAN RIJN REMBRANDT

VOCABULARY: portrait, body language, intrigue.

MATERIALS: water color paints, or colored pencil, or crayons, paper, pencil.

ACTIVITY:

1.   Study some of the works of Rembrandt.

2.   Like Rembrandt, you will draw or paint a portrait of yourself or someone you know very well.

3.   Give your audience clues about the person in the portrait. Use facial expression, body language, color, and props in your portrait.

4.   The props should be items like clothing, hats, jewelry, furniture, tea cups, and so forth, that define the person in the portrait.

5.   Have fun setting up the portrait with the props. Remember lighting can affect the portrait, too. Will the portrait be dark or full of bright light? Sign the portrait when it is completed.

Evaluation   Name _____

THINKING ABOUT HARMENSZOON VAN RIJN REMBRANDT AND ME

Respond to four or more of the following questions/statements:

1. Who did you paint or draw a portrait of, and why?

2. Explain the facial expressions or body language you used in your painting or drawing.

3. Describe and explain the meaning of some of the props you used in your painting or drawing.

4. Explain how Rembrandt's portraits make you feel. Do they intrigue you, make you happy or sad? Write an explanation in your own words.

5. Pretend you were alive when Rembrandt was living, and he asked you to pose for a portrait. How would you dress and how would you want Rembrandt to portray you?

6. Write one or more paragraphs about what you have learned about this artist and/or what you have learned through your own creative project relating to this artist. Write this information on the opposite side of this sheet, or on a separate sheet of paper.

Georges Seurat
(zhawrzh) (suh RAH)
1859-1891

Georges Seurat devoted most of his artistic energy to seven very large and monumental paintings. One of his most famous oil paintings, hanging in The Art Institute of Chicago, is entitled *Sunday Afternoon on the Island of La Grand Jatte*. This painting measures a little over six feet nine inches in height and it is ten feet in length. The painting shows us many people strolling through a park, lounging on the grass, and watching the sailboats and rowboats on the water. Seurat painted this picture only after he had done many studies and sketches for it and one of these drawings, *Tree on the Bank of the Seine*, done with conté crayon, also hangs in The Art Institute of Chicago. This simple drawing shows us how carefully Seurat studied the tree forms he wanted to include in his *La Grande Jatte* painting. The trees almost look bare in this preliminary study, but Seurat was aware of the figures he would later place in *La Grande Jatte*.

This masterpiece took two years for Seurat to paint and the island of La Grand Jatte became the setting for several of his paintings. In addition to his masterpiece *La Grande Jatte*, Seurat is perhaps most famous for his innovative painting procedures in which he used tiny brushstrokes of contrasting color to portray the play of light. Seurat called his procedure "Divisionism," but the method is more frequently known as "Pointillism." The very many tiny spots of color dotting his canvas gave his paintings a shimmering effect.

Georges Seurat was born in Paris on December 2, 1859, to Ernestine Faivre and Antoine-Chrisostôme Seurat, a property owner. Georges spent most of his childhood in Paris living with his mother, his brother Emile, and his sister Marie-Berthe. When Georges was in school he began to draw, and when he was sixteen years old, he took a course from a sculptor. He later studied painting at the École des Beaux-Arts. His teacher there was Henri Lehmann, a disciple of Ingres, who was a great portraitist. Georges became fascinated with the relationship between lines and images and their aesthetic (or beautiful) appeal.

In 1879, after a year of military service in Brest, Seurat returned to Paris and shared a studio with another painter, Edmond-François Aman-Jean, who also studied with Henri Lehmann. In 1883, Seurat displayed portraits of his mother and his friend Aman-Jean at the official Salon, an annual state-sponsored exhibit of artists' works. In the same year, Seurat began working on his first large-scale painting, *Une Baignade, Asniéres*, and exhibited this painting in 1884 with the Société des Artistes Indépendents. When Seurat exhibited La Grande Jatte at an Impressionist Group Show in 1886, his technique using

Pointillism generated a lot of enthusiasm and interest. Two of Seurat's disciples, his artistic followers or pupils, were Camille Pissaro and Paul Signac, artists who became famous in their own right and who were also interested in the effects of light on color.

Seurat's final composition on the large scale of *Baignade* and *La Grande Jatte* was *Les Poseuses*. After *Les Poseuses* was completed in 1888, Seurat painted a number of landscapes and portraits and he continued to show his work in various exhibitions in Paris and Brussels.

In February of 1890, a son was born to Seurat and Madeleine Knobloch, the woman with whom Seurat lived. While organizing an exhibition of paintings at the eighth Salon des Indépendents where he showed what was to be his last painting, *Le Cirque*, Seurat became exhausted. He caught a chill and developed infectious angina. Seurat died on March 29, 1891, on Easter Sunday, before the exhibition ended. Seurat's year old son contracted his father's illness and died a few weeks after his father's death.

Though Georges Seurat's artistic career was relatively brief, his work and the theories behind his work show us that he was one of the foremost painters in one of the greatest periods in the history of art. He took brilliant colors and effects of sunlight, two important characteristics of Impressionism, one step further. He created Pointillism by covering his canvas with a mass of colorful dots that seemed to make his paintings flicker with beautiful light and dreamlike haziness.

GEORGES SEURAT

VOCABULARY: pointillism, image, investigate, sparse, illustrate.

MATERIALS: fine point colored markers, unlined index cards, pencil.

ACTIVITY:

1. Study photographs of Georges Seurat's paintings.

2. Although Georges Seurat painted paintings, not name tags, you will make a name tag or gift tag in the style of Seurat's pointillism.

3. Fold your index card in half lengthwise.

4. Choose the image you want on the card and draw it lightly in pencil first. Then, use your fine point markers to add the dots.

5. Put the dots of various colors where you think they should be. You can also vary the size of your dots and the amount of space between them. Sign your name tag.

Evaluation   Name _____

THINKING ABOUT GEORGES SEURAT AND ME

Respond to four or more of the following questions/statements:

1. Investigate and explain the difference between areas with a sparse amount of dots and areas with large masses of dots.

2. Evaluate how your tag looks up close and how it looks far away. Which way do you prefer to look at it? Explain:

3. How will you use your tag and why?

4. Suppose everything in real life looked like pointillism. Would you like that? Why?

5. Pretend you are Georges Seurat. Explain why you work with dots.

6. Write one or more paragraphs about what you have learned about this artist and/or what you have learned through your own creative project relating to this artist. Write this information on the opposite side of this sheet, or on a separate sheet of paper.

Vincent van Gogh
1853-1890

Yellow was the favorite color of the Dutch-born master of the Post-Impressionist period, Vincent van Gogh, and perhaps it is because of his love for the color yellow, that he worshipped the warm and vibrant sun and all its vivid colors, ranging from fiery orange to bright lemon-yellow. Even the sunflowers in his famous paintings look like small sunbursts in their yellow vase atop a yellow table.

Vincent van Gogh was born on March 30, 1853, in Groot-Zundert, North Brabant, Holland. His father was a pastor there and the family lived modestly. Vincent was the eldest child in the family consisting of several younger brothers and sisters as well, and even as a young boy, he displayed signs of unusual character that often worried his parents. Often times Vincent was very unsociable and undisciplined. Vincent had a younger brother, Theo, four years his junior, to whom he was very close. Theo was always very supportive of Vincent, and it was Theo who first encouraged Vincent to become a painter.

When Vincent was sixteen years old, in 1869, he obtained a position in the Goupil firm of art dealers, where his uncle was employed. Vincent first worked at the firm's branch in The Hague, and then later in Brussels. While he worked at Goupil, packing and unpacking paintings and books, he had the opportunity to visit many museums and read many books.

Vincent worked for several years in Goupil's London branch and then in their Paris branch. He was becoming intensely involved in religion, and when he lost his job in Paris, he returned to London to work as a lay preacher in a church school. After spending a short time with his parents, Vincent decided to move to Amsterdam to study theology. He wanted to become a pastor and especially help those who were very unfortunate. When Vincent failed to pass the theological examination, he began, instead, to train as a missionary. He was sent to work in the Borinage, a coal-mining district, helping the poor miners there. In the Borinage, Vincent gave away everything he owned. He slept on dirt floors, wore no socks, and made his shirts out of old pack-cloth. Even though Vincent was very weak and thin from exhaustion and hunger, he took care of the tired and sick coal miners, too. Other clergymen thought Vincent had gone too far in his zeal to help the poor and sick, so he was dismissed from his job.

Sad because he had failed as a preacher and missionary, Vincent turned to drawing and painting. He was helped and encouraged by his brother, Theo, who was now working for the Goupil art firm. Vincent studied the works of J.F. Millet,

Rubens, and several Japanese artists, including Hokusai. He drew the coal miners of the Borinage, landscapes of cornfields, vases of flowers, and many self portraits. He tried to study art very seriously at the Academy of Art in Antwerp. In 1886, Vincent moved to Paris to live with Theo. There he met many of the Impressionist painters including Lautrec, Pissaro, Degas, and Gauguin. Vincent and Gauguin became friends and in 1888, when Vincent moved to Arles, in the south of France, Gauguin came to live with him for a short while.

While in Arles, Vincent was very productive. He rented a small house, painting it yellow and naming it the "House of Friends." There he worked at his paintings all day long. In the fifteen months he lived in Arles, he produced over two hundred paintings. While Vincent was very happy painting in Arles, he was also beginning to suffer from bad hallucinations. When Gauguin visited Vincent, Vincent – in a state of dementia – cut off his own ear after quarreling with Gauguin. Because he was becoming more and more mentally unbalanced, Vincent agreed to be hospitalized. Even when Vincent was in the hospital, he painted constantly. In his paintings during this period, one can see the bright colors Vincent loved, wriggling across the canvas, conveying perhaps his restlessness and intensity of emotion.

In 1890, the art critic Albert Aurier wrote about Vincent's work in an article of the *Mercure de France*. After this publication, Vincent sold his first and only painting during his lifetime. Then, after a brief visit to Paris in May of 1890, Vincent moved to Auvers-sur-Oise and placed himself under the care of Dr. Gachet, a friend of many Impressionist painters. Vincent's portrait of Dr. Gachet is now very famous.

On July 27, 1890, because he was very ill, Vincent shot himself. He died two days later, and his beloved bother, Theo, died six months later. Both of them are buried in the little churchyard cemetery of Auvers.

Vincent van Gogh painted many masterpieces of nature and humanity. He was very sensitive to the plight and misery of those less fortunate, and because of his own mental illness, he was always seeking calming light and peace. His brilliant landscapes, still lifes, and portraits often bring the quiet joy of light and peace to those who view them. Van Gogh sold only one painting in his brief and unhappy life. It is ironic that his painting, *Portrait of Dr. Gachet*, sold to a Japanese art gallery for over eighty million dollars in May of 1990, then the highest price ever paid for a painting in the modern world.

VINCENT van GOGH

VOCABULARY: impasto, self-portrait, subject matter, vibrant, emotion.

MATERIALS: tempera or poster paints, white school glue, paint brushes, posterboard (cut in 8 x 10, 9 x 12, or 11 x 14 inch sizes), paper cups.

ACTIVITY:

1. Study some of the various works of Vincent van Gogh.

2. Pour tempera or poster paint color into a cup. Fill each cup half full. Then add equal parts of glue to each color cup. Mix well. The paint will be thick like the paint that van Gogh used in some of this paintings.

3. Choose a posterboard that you would like to work on. Then decide on your subject matter. Will you choose to paint a landscape or a self-portrait?

4. If you choose a landscape, work outside or look outside. If you choose to do a self-portrait, sit in front of a mirror to look at yourself. As you look into the mirror, try to capture your facial features. Perhaps you might want to draw your features before you paint them.

5. Think about the vibrant color and the thick brush stroke that van Gogh used. Think about van Gogh's energetic brush strokes as you paint. Like van Gogh, try to put a lot of emotion in your painting.

THINKING ABOUT VINCENT van GOGH AND ME

Respond to four or more of the following questions/statements:

1. Describe what you were feeling when you were painting your picture.

2. Do you think that any of your emotions show in your painting? Explain:

3. If you chose to paint a landscape, what kind of brushstrokes did you use for the sky, clouds, grass, and the trees? If you chose to do a self-portrait, how did you portray yourself? For example, do you look sad, happy, surprised, or solemn in your portrait? Write your answer in a complete sentence.

4. Explain how you feel about the painting style of van Gogh.

5. If van Gogh had lived longer, what do you think he might have painted for his next three masterpieces? Tell why you think he might have chosen those pictures to paint.

6. Write one or more paragraphs about what you have learned about this artist and/or what you have learned through your own creative project relating to this artist. Write this information on the opposite side of this sheet, or on a separate sheet of paper.

Frank Lloyd Wright
1867-1959

Frank Lloyd Wright was one of America's most important and imaginative architects. For nearly seventy years, he designed many unusual homes and buildings, including the Robie and Cheney houses in Illinois, his own home – Taliesin – near Spring Green, Wisconsin, the Guggenheim Museum in New York City, and the Imperial Hotel in Tokyo, Japan. Wright even designed a one mile high skyscraper by the shore of Lake Michigan.

Frank Lloyd Wright was born in Richland Center, Wisconsin, in 1867, and spent his youth in the valley of the Wisconsin River where he was first inspired by the surrounding prairie. When he was ready for college, in the mid 1880s, Wright briefly studied engineering at the University of Wisconsin. In 1887, when he was twenty years old, Wright moved to Chicago where he worked as a draftsman for Joseph Lyman Silsbee, a famous Midwestern architect, before joining the staff of the famous Chicago architects Dankmar Adler and Louis H. Sullivan. Louis H. Sullivan is considered America's first modern architect and he was responsible for designing the first skyscraper in 1894 in Buffalo, New York. Sullivan believed that an architect "was a poet who used materials, rather than words" and he was a great influence on the young Wright.

Wright shared many valuable architectural principles and philosophies with Sullivan and Wright believed, like his mentor, Sullivan, that the form of a building should follow its function or purpose, and that a building should reflect the personality and characteristics of its inhabitants. Both architects believed that the interior design and decor of a building should harmoniously reflect the outside of a building.

In 1893, Wright established his own architectural practice and went on to design many homes and buildings in the Chicago area. Nature played a very vital role in all of Wright's designs and Wright found that nature was the one perennial source for his architectural inspirations. Wright liked to use strong building materials such as stone, wood, brick, glass, copper, concrete, and steel because of the variety and texture in those materials. He disliked paint and wallpaper because they masked the natural colors and patterns of those building materials. The living spaces of the early American Indians and the traditional Japanese also greatly influenced Wright's work because their dwellings were so attuned to their natural surroundings.

The common buildings of the prairie – barns, silos, sheds, and windmills – influenced Wright's homes designed in his famous "prairie style." These very open and spacious prairie style homes were low to the ground and horizontal in shape and there was much use of glass – large, long ranges of windows, doors, and porches – so that the building was open to the landscape, and nature became the primary ornament of the house.

Wright was very aware of the three-dimensional aspects in his buildings and he was conscious of the visual and structural relationship between vertical and horizontal shapes. He also made much use of cantilevers – large horizontal beams extending outward over space – in his designs. He believed that cantilevers freed rooms from traditional confining shapes and he made cantilevers the main instrument for asserting new freedom in architecture.

One of the last projects Wright designed, and one of his most famous, was the Guggenheim Museum, completed in 1960, in New York City. Wright designed the Guggenheim so that its space looked like one continuous curve, almost like an unbroken wave. Inside the museum there is a dominating spiral ramp that runs from the floor almost to the ceiling.

Frank Lloyd Wright believed that the buildings he designed had a profound influence on the people inside them. Perhaps it is because of his acute awareness of the inhabitants of his buildings, and his blending of buildings with their surrounding environments, that his unique and unusual designs remain so important and famous today.

Name _____

FRANK LLOYD WRIGHT

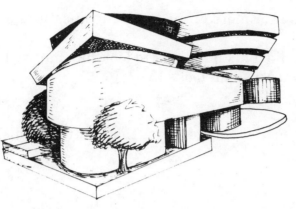

VOCABULARY: architect, reinforced concrete, steel, cantilever, three-dimensional.

MATERIALS FOR TWO-DIMENSIONAL DRAWING: paper, pencil, markers, or crayons.

MATERIALS FOR THREE-DIMENSIONAL BUILDING: shoebox, paper, pencil, markers and/or crayons, glue, scissors.

ACTIVITY:

1.   Study some of the works of Frank Lloyd Wright, including the Guggenheim museum that he designed.

2.   Pretend that you are Frank Lloyd Wright. Draw the Guggenheim Museum, or reconstruct it with a shoebox and paper.

3.   Try to do the best you can to make your museum look like the Guggenheim. Remember some of the interesting ideas that Frank Lloyd Wright had as he constructed it:

   A. The inside of a building should look like the outside, and the outside should look like the inside.

   B. Mr. Wright liked to think that architecture should resemble forms in nature.

   C. Mr. Wright liked his buildings to look as if they grew where they had been built.

Evaluation   Name ——————————————————————

THINKING ABOUT FRANK LLOYD WRIGHT AND ME

Respond to four or more of the following questions/statements:

1. Since Mr. Wright liked his buildings to look like nature forms, what do you think the Guggenheim Museum looks like?

Try to think of at least three things, other than nature forms, that the Guggenheim resembles.

2. Do you think that the Guggenheim is a good design for a museum? Explain:

3. Did you have any problems designing your building? Explain the problems you had, or if you didn't have any problems, what did you do to prevent them?

4. How would you have made the museum different from Mr. Wright's museum building if you had been building it?

5. If you draw or construct a building of your own, how will it be better and different from any other building that you have seen?

6. Write one or more paragraphs about what you have learned about this artist and/or what you have learned through your own creative project relating to this artist. Write this information on the opposite side of this sheet, or on a separate sheet of paper.

MUSEUM/GALLERY VISIT REPORT FORM

Your Name _____ Teacher _____

NAME & LOCATION OF MUSEUM/GALLERY: _____

_____

DATE OF VISIT: _____

ARTIST'S NAME: _____

DATE OF WORK: _____

TITLE: (if there is one) _____

MATERIALS: (medium) _____

Describe what you see:

What "feelings" does this piece give you? Does it affect your feelings/senses in any way? Describe:

If you had to grade or rate this piece of artwork on a scale of 1 to 10, what score would you give it and why? Circle the score: 1 2 3 4 5 6 7 8 9 10

Name _____

BIOGRAPHY/AUTOBIOGRAPHY
(of an artist outside of this book)

ARTIST: _____

TITLE OF BOOK: _____

PUBLISHER: _____

WHERE DOES (OR DID) THIS ARTIST LIVE? _____

_____

WHAT MEDIUM OR MEDIA DOES (OR DID) THIS ARTIST USE? _____

_____

Write at least three interesting things you have learned about the artist from your readings:

Explain why this person became famous:

Name three or more titles or descriptions of work by this artist:

Name _____

CREATIVE ART PROJECT
(for independent learning)

MATERIALS NEEDED: _____

_____

PLANS FOR CREATIVE PROJECT: _____

_____

_____

_____

ADULT APPROVAL: _____

Did you have any problems in creating your project? Why or why not?

What did you learn from creating this project that will help you do better on your next similar project?

Make a sketch of your finished project and write a brief description of it.

READ TO DISCOVER INFORMATION ABOUT A DIFFERENT ARTIST

Artist ————————————— Name —————————————

MEDIA MATERIALS
Find and read at least three sources about the artist:

Title of Media	Where it was obtained

OTHER INFORMATION DISCOVERED ABOUT THE ARTIST

————————————————————————————————

————————————————————————————————

————————————————————————————————

————————————————————————————————

————————————————————————————————

————————————————————————————————

————————————————————————————————

————————————————————————————————

GLOSSARY

accent – to stress or emphasize something in an art form.

Action Painting – a painting method and movement where the paint is flung and thrown onto the canvas. The paint becomes "active" in the painting process.

aesthetic – to understand an artwork with your senses, such as sight, hearing, taste, touch, and smell. Pleasing beauty in art.

architect – an artist who combines design and science to create buildings and homes.

aspirations – dreams of higher achievements and goals.

asymmetry – something that is unbalanced or uneven.

body language – using the human body to suggest emotion and to communicate through posture and action.

cantilever – a modern architectural structure where a beam is supported at one end and the other end is projected outward. It was developed by Frank Lloyd Wright.

canvas board – cardboard that has canvas glued to it and which is used as a painting surface.

chalkpastel – a stick made up of powdered color and glue.

close-up – a view of an object or person that is focused at a very short distance.

collage – an art form where pieces or pictures of objects are pasted together.

component – a part, or an ingredient in something.

contrast – to show differences between objects.

create – to make, to produce.

delicate – very fragile, or having fine qualities.

depth – space or distance.

design – the form or shape of a thing.

detail – a specific, or a particular part of something.

distort – to change something or someone so it does not resemble the way it appears in real life.

drama – a showing of excitement and action.

droughts – a severe or serious shortage of rain and moisture that leads to land and crop damage.

emotion – a personal feeling, such as sadness.

emotional release – a chance to express or free your feelings.

engineer – a planner of structures, machines, or systems.

engraving – a system of printmaking where the image is cut into a metal plate with sharp tools. Ink is then rubbed on the plate into the cut grooves. Paper is applied on the plate and run through a press. The image is pressed onto the paper.

express – to convey a thought, feeling, or opinion.

figure – a shape that represents the human form.

folk artist – an artist who has had no formal art training.

footbridge – a bridge for people to walk over, usually over a small body of water.

gallery – a shop where art work is displayed for sale.

gesture – a movement that suggests an emotion.

Great Depression – a time span during the 1930s in American history where the economy was in serious trouble and many people lost all of their money.

hidden meaning – a message or definition that is not easily seen or understood.

high value – a color that has much white added to it, or a work of art that has much light in it.

illustrate – to draw a picture that shows something, or tells a story.

image – a replica or copy of a person, place, or thing.

impasto – thick paint that is applied to the painting with a brush or a palette knife and which gives the surface of the painting a rough texture.

Impressionism – a movement in art that emphasized color, light, and emotion rather than detail.

inspired – to be moved with creative energy.

intrigue – to fascinate, to spark curiosity.

investigate – to research, to study.

landscape painting – a painting with the outdoors as its subject.

low value – a color that has much black added to it, or a work of art that has more darkness than lightness in it.

manila/newsprint paper – an inexpensive paper used for sketching and drawing, usually beige or yellow in color.

mass – weight, bulk.

masterpiece – an artwork that was completed with a skill that is of superior quality.

medium – the raw materials used in creating a work of art.

mobile – a linear hanging sculpture that moves. It was invented by Alexander Calder.

motif – theme or subject.

motion – movement, action.

mural – a large painting or drawing usually done on a wall.

mystery – something that is not able to be understood or solved.

negative space – the "holes" or space left by the form or positive space.

organic – resembling a living thing.

pastel color – a soft, lighter color with much white added to it.

peaceable kingdom – an area of space containing harmony, peace, and calm.

plight – a problem or bad condition.

Pointillism – a style of painting and drawing invented by Georges Seurat where dots of color are put on the art work's surface and which blend into each other when viewed from a distance.

portrait – a painting, drawing, or photograph that represents a person, real or fictitious.

positive space – the space of the actual form.

precise – exact, perfect.

proverbs – a saying or statement that is short and has a useful and wise meaning.

Quakers – English people who came to America to find religious freedom. They wore simple clothes, spoke a simple language, and believed all people were equals.

realism – in the visual arts, work that represents real life.

recede – to go back in space.

reflection – an image that is mirrored in a shiny surface.

reinforced concrete – concrete that is strengthened by having metal in it.

rhythmic – anything patterned with movement or a beat.

rural – referring to the countryside's land or people.

scene – the place or location where something occurs.

sculpture – three dimensional art work, such as Henry Moore's work. Moore was a sculptor because he made sculpture.

signature – a handwritten personal name.

simplified – made easier, uncomplicated.

sketch – a fast drawing without careful details.

social problems – distressing situations pertaining to people, such as homelessness.

socially conscious – relating to issues or problems of people.

solidity – the state of having weight and substance.

space – an area that is unoccupied or empty.

sparse – a small and irregular amount.

steel – a mixture of iron and carbon that forms a powerful metal.

still life – in the visual arts, subject matter that is not living, such as apples or chairs.

suspense – a feeling of not knowing what the outcome of a situation will be.

symbol – an object or person that stands for something or someone else.

symmetry – something that is balanced or even.

technique – the way something is done, or how something is applied.

texture – the surface feeling or look of an object.

three dimensional – any object having height, width, and depth.

verse – written lines found in poems or in the Bible.

vibrant – intensely bright or vivid.

wo/man – an abbreviation for woman an/or man.

ARTIST BIBLIOGRAPHY

CALDER, ALEXANDER

Lipman, Jean and
  Margaret Aspinwall
Alexander Calder and his Magical Mobiles. New York: Hudson Hills Press, 1981.

Parish, Peggy
Beginning Mobiles. (Calder) Illustrated by Lynn Sweat. New York: Macmillan Publishing Co., Inc., 1979.

CASSATT, MARY

Epstein, Vivian S.
History of Women Artists for Children. Denver, CO: VSE Publisher, 1989. (page 16)

Meyer, Susan
First Impressions: Mary Cassatt. New York, New York. Harry Abrams Publishers, 1990.

Venezia, Mike
Getting to Know the World's Greatest Artists: Mary Cassatt. Chicago: Childrens Press, 1991.

CÉZANNE, PAUL

Kaufman, Elizabeth
Cézanne. Secaucus, N. J.: Castle Books, Ottenheimer Publishers, 1980.

Ventura, Piero
Great Painters. New York: G. P. Putnam's Sons, 1984. (page 132)

CHAGALL, MARC

Greenfeld, Howard
First Impressions: Marc Chagall. New York, New York. Harry Abrams Publishers, 1990.

Raboff, Ernest
Marc Chagall. Art for Children. New York: Harper & Row, Publishers, 1988.

DEGAS, EDGAR

Woold, Felicity
Picture This (A First Introduction to Paintings). New York: Doubleday, 1989. (page 27)

Newlands, Anne
Meet Edgar Degas. (National Gallery of Canada) New York: J. B. Lippincott, 1988.

DÜRER, ALBRECHT

Raboff, Ernest
Albrecht Dürer. Art for Children. New York: Harper & Row, Publishers, 1988.

HICKS, EDWARD

Sullivan, Charles
  edited by

Imaginary Gardens: American Poetry and Art for Young People.
New York: Harry N. Abrams, Inc., 1989.

Durell, Ann and
  Marilyn Sachs
  edited by
Bierhorst, Jane Byers
  designed by

The Big Book for Peace. New York: Dutton Children's Books,
1990.

HOMER, WINSLOW

Homer, Winslow

Winslow Homer Illustrations. New York: Dover Publications,
1983.

Sullivan, Charles
  edited by

Imaginary Gardens: American Poetry and Art for Young People.
New York: Harry N. Abrams, Inc., 1989.

Koch, Kenneth and
  Kate Farrell

*Talking to the Sun – An Illustrated Anthology of Poems for Young
People.* New York: The Metropolitan Museum of Art, Henry Holt
Company, 1985.

LANGE, DOROTHEA

Blumenfeld, Milton

Careers in Photography. Minneapolis: Lerner Publications
Company, 1979.

Freeman, Tony

A New True Book. Photography. Prepared under the direction of
Illa Podendorf. Chicago: Childrens Press, 1983.

Meltzer, Milton

Dorothea Lange – Life Through the Camera. New York: Viking
Kestral, Viking Penguin, Inc., 1985.

MATISSE, HENRI

Munthe, Nelly

Meet Matisse. Boston: Little, Brown and Company, 1983.

Raboff, Ernest

Henri Matisse. Art for Children. New York: Harper & Row,
Publishers, 1988.

MONET, CLAUDE

Bjork, Christina

Linnea in Monet's Garden. Drawings by Lena Anderson. New
York: R & S Books, 1985. Fiction.

Venezia, Mike

Getting to Know the World's Greatest Artists: Monet. Chicago:
Childrens Press, 1990.

Ventura, Piero

Great Painters. New York: G. P. Putnam's Sons, 1984. (page 132)

MOORE, HENRY

Baylor, Byrd

When Clay Sings. Illustrated by Tom Bahti. New York: Aladdin Books, Macmillan Publishing Company, 1972.

Kohl, Mary Ann

Mudworks – Creative Clay, Dough and Modeling Experiences. Bellingham, WA: Bright Ring Publishing, 1989.

Thompson, Susan C.

Hooray for Clay! Photographs by Tom Smucker, Drawings by William Conklin, Jr. and clay figures by Susan Conklin Thompson. Unique Clay Activities for Young Children. (K-2) Glenview, IL: Scott, Foresman, 1989.

MOSES, ANNA MARY ROBERTSON (GRANDMA MOSES)

O'Neal, Zibby

Grandma Moses, Painter of Rural America. Illustrations by Donna Ruff, Paintings by Grandma Moses. New York: Puffin Books, 1986.

Sullivan, Charles
edited by

Imaginary Gardens: American Poetry and Art for Young People. New York: Harry N. Abrams, Inc., 1989.

O'KEEFFE GEORGIA

Epstein, Vivian S.

History of Women Artists for Children. Denver, CO: VSE Publisher, 1989. (page 17)

Geherman, Beverly

Georgia O'Keeffe, The "Wilderness and Wonder" of Her World. New York: Macmillan, 1986.

Sills, Leslie

Inspirations: Stories About Women Artists. Georgia O'Keeffe, Frida Kahlo, Alice Neel, Faith Ringgold. Niles, IL: Albert Whitman & Company, 1989.

POLLOCK, JACKSON

Woolf, Felicity

Picture This (A First Introduction to Paintings). New York: Doubleday, 1989. (pages 32 and 33)

Koch, Kenneth and
Kate Farrell

Talking to the Sun-An Illustrated Anthology of Poems for Young People. New York: The Metropolitan Museum of Art, Henry Holt and Company, 1985.

REMBRANDT, HARMENSZOON VAN RIJN

Raboff, Ernest
Rembrandt. Art for Children. New York: Harper & Row, Publishers, 1987.

Strand, Mark
Rembrandt Takes a Walk. Illustrations by Red Grooms. New York: Clarkson N. Potter Publishers (Distributed by Crown Publishers), 1986.

Venezia, Mike
Getting to Know the World's Greatest Artists: Rembrandt. Chicago Childrens Press, 1988.

SEURAT, GEORGES

Hallowell, Bay with
Amy Kellman and
Barbara Lucas
Art Ventures (A Guide for Families to Impressionism and Post-Impressionism). Illustrated by Edward Koren. Pittsburgh, PA: The Carnegie Museum of Art, 1989. Publication made possible by Ford Motor Company.

Ventura, Piero
Great Painters. New York: G. P. Putnam's Sons, 1984. (page 132)

VAN GOGH, VINCENT

Raboff, Ernest
Van Gogh. (Art for Children). New York: Harper & Row, 1987.

Uhde, W.
Van Gogh. New York: Phaidon, 1951. 11th Edition 1972.

Venezia, Mike
Getting to Know the World's Greatest Artists: Van Gogh. Chicago: Childrens Press, 1988.

WRIGHT, FRANK LLOYD

Hoffman, Donald
Frank Lloyd Wright. Architecture and Nature. New York: Dover Publications, Inc., 1986.

Isaacson, Philip
Round Buildings, Square Buildings, & Buildings That Wiggle Like a Fish. New York: Alfred A. Knopf, 1988.

Maddex, Diane
Architects Make Zigzags (Looking at Architecture from A to Z). Drawings by Roxie Munro. Washington, D. C.: The Preservation Press, 1986.

PICTURE BOOK BIBLIOGRAPHY

dePaola, Tomie   *The Art Lesson*. New York: G. P. Putnam's Sons, 1989.

dePaola, Tomie   *The Legend of the Indian Paintbrush*. New York: G. P. Putnam's Sons, 1988.

Emberley, Rebecca   *Drawing with Numbers and Letters*. Boston: Little, Brown and Company, 1981.

Freeman, Don   *Norman the Doorman*. (Sculpture, Fiction) New York: Puffin Books, 1959. Reprinted 1987.

Goffstein, M. B.   *An Artist's Album*. New York: Harper and Row/Charlotte Zolotow Books, 1985.

Goffstein, M. B.   *Artists' Helpers Enjoy the Evenings*. New York: Harper and Row/ Charlotte Zolotow Books, 1987.

Kesselman, Wendy   *Emma*. Illustrated by Barbara Cooney. New York: Harper & Row, 1980.

Levy, Virginia K.   *Let's Go to the Art Museum*. New York: Harry N. Abrams, 1988.

Ryland, Cynthia   *All I See*. Pictures by Peter Catallanotto. New York: Orchard Books, 1988.

Testa, Fulvio   *If You Look Around You*. New York: Dial Press, 1983.

Testa, Fulvio   *If You Take a Paintbrush (A Book Of Colors)*. New York: Dial Press, 1982.

Testa, Fulvio   *If You Take a Pencil*. New York: Dial Press, 1982.

Walsh, Ellen Stoll   *Mouse Paint*. San Diego, CA: Harcourt Brace Jovanovich, 1989.

Willard, Nancy   *Simple Pictures are Best*. Pictures by Tomie de Paola. New York: Harcourt Brace Jovanovich, 1976.

BOOKS FOR PARENTS AND TEACHERS

Brooks, Susan W. and Susan M. Senatori	*SEE THE PAINTINGS! (A Handbook for Art Appreciation in the Classroom)*, Rosemont, New Jersey. Modern Learning Press, 1988.
Edwards, Betty	*Drawing on the Artist Within*. New York: Simon and Schuster, 1986.
Edwards, Betty	*Drawing on the Right Side of the Brain*. Los Angeles: J. P. Tarcher, 1979.
Warner, Sally	*Encouraging the Artist in Your Child (Even If You Can't Draw)*. Line Illustrations by Sally Warner. Kids' illustrations by Alex, Andrew, Cassandra, Evan, Nico, and Anna. Photographs by Claire Henze. New York: St. Martin's Press, 1989.
Wilson, Marjorie and Brent	*Teaching Children to Draw: A Guide for Teachers and Parents*. Englewood Cliffs, NJ: Prentice-Hall, 1982.

OTHER FINE ART BOOKS

Arnosky, Jim — *Drawing From Nature*. New York: Lothrop, Lee and Shepard Books, 1987.

Arnosky, Jim — *Drawing Life in Motion*. New York: Lothrop, Lee and Shepard Books, 1984.

Brown, Laurene and Marc Brown — *Visiting the Art Museum*. New York: E. P. Dutton, 1986.

Ceserani, Gian — *Grand Constructions*. Illustrated by Piero Ventura. New York: G. P. Putnam's Sons, 1983.

Clinton, Susan — *I Can Be An Architect*. Prepared under the direction of Robert Hillerich, Ph. D. Chicago: Children Press, 1986.

Conner, Patrick — *People at Home (Looking at Art Series)*. New York: Atheneum, 1982. (a Margaret K. McElderry Book)

D'Alelio, Jane — *I Know That Building! Discovering Architecture with Activities and Games*. New York: The Preservation Press, 1989.

Farrell, Kate — *People*. New York: The Metropolitan Museum of Art, Henry Holt and Company, 1985.

Hallowell, Bay with Amy Kellman and Barbara Lucas — *Art Ventures (A Guide for Families to Impressionism and Post-Impressionism)*. Illustrations by Edward Koren. Pittsburgh, PA: The Carnegie Museum of Art, 1989. Publication made possible by Ford Motor Company.

Kohl, Mary Ann — *Scribble Cookies (and other Independent Creative Art Experiences for Children)*. Illustrated by Judy McCoy. Bellingham, WA: Bright Ring Publishing, 1985.

Locker, Thomas — *The Young Artist*. New York: Dial Books, 1989.

Maril, Nadja — *Me, Molly Midnight the artist's cat*. Paintings and drawings by Herman Maril. Owings Mills, MD: Stemmer House, 1977.

Mayers, Florence C. — *The Museum of Modern Art, New York . ABC*. New York: Harry N. Abrams, Inc. 1986.

Mayers, Florence C. — *Museum of Fine Arts, Boston ABC*. New York: Harry N. Abrams, Inc., 1986.

Peppin, Anthea — *The Usborne Story of Painting*. Illustrated by Joseph McEwan, Edited by Robyn Gee. Tulsa, OK: Hayes Books, 1980.

Robbins, Ken — *Building a House*. New York: Four Winds Press, 1984.

Sibley, Brian   *The Pooh Sketchbook*. Drawings by Ernest H. Shepard for the Pooh stories by A. A. Milne. New York: E. P. Dutton, 1984.

Simon, Hilda   *The Magic of Color*. New York: Lothrop, Lee and Shepard, 1981.

Tofts, Hannah   *The Print Book – Fun Things to Make and Do with Print*. New York: Simon and Schuster, 1990.

Tofts, Hannah   *The 3-D Paper Book – Fun Things to Make and Do with Paper*. New York: Simon and Schuster, 1990.

Tofts, Hannah   *The Paper Book – Fun Things to Make and Do with Paper*. New York: Simon and Schuster, 1990.

Tofts, Hannah   *The Paint Book – Fun Things to Make and Do with Paint*. New York: Simon and Schuster, 1990.

Waterfield, Giles   *Faces (Looking at Art Series)*. New York: Atheneum, 1982. (a Margaret K. McElderry Book)

Wilson, Forrest   *What It Feels Like to be a Building*. Washington, D.C.: The Preservation Press, 1988.

PARENT/TEACHER NOTES

T.S. Denison & Co., Inc.   102   *Let's Meet Famous Artists*

PARENT/TEACHER NOTES

THE AUTHORS

Harriet Kinghorn

Harriet Kinghorn has taught preschool, kindergarten, and grades two through four in elementary schools in Nebraska and Minnesota. She holds the degrees Bachelor of Science and Master of Science in Education. She is presently teaching enrichment classes in the elementary schools in East Grand Forks, Minnesota. Harriet has stories, games, unit and art activities published in various education magazines. She has also written and published numerous activity books, such as four books, entitled *Independent Activities*, and eight books with Robert King, entitled *Storytime Classics* published by T. S. Denison. Harriet was honored as one of twelve "Honor Teachers of Minnesota" in 1976.

Jacqueline Badman

Jacqueline Badman was born and raised in Schenectady, New York. She attended State University of New York at Purchase where she graduated magna cum laude with a Bachelor of Fine Arts Degree. Jacqueline then moved to Grand Forks, North Dakota, to do graduate work in painting and drawing at the University of North Dakota. She teaches Introduction to Fine Arts part-time for the University of North Dakota's Continuing Education Program. She also works at Dunahey's Art and Learning Center where she continually meets artists and teachers. With her jewelry designer husband, David, she co-owns their business Studio 18/Badman Enterprises and markets his jewelry across the country.

This is Jacqueline's first book. Her love of art, children, and writing has made it enjoyable to co-author with Harriet and Lisa.

Lisa Lewis-Spicer

Lisa Lewis-Spicer received her Master of Arts in English from the University of North Dakota where she has been a lecturer for six years, specializing in writing classes centered on *The New Yorker* magazine.

She has lived in Italy and Egypt and she has traveled extensively, visiting many museums and galleries, and recently exploring with two of her children the museums in London.

Lisa and her husband, Mark, have four young children who spend many moments reading and drawing and inspiring their parents.